THE NECESSARY GOODBYE

PETER D. BANKO

THE NECESSARY GOODBYE

HOW GREAT LEADERS FIRE WITH CLARITY, CONFIDENCE, AND COMPASSION

Forbes | Books

Published by Forbes Books, Charleston, South Carolina.
An imprint of Advantage Media Group.

Printed in the United States of America.

10 9 8 7 6 5 4 3 2 1

ISBN: 979-8-88750-812-2 (Hardcover)
ISBN: 979-8-88750-813-9 (eBook)
ISBN: 979-888750-814-6 (Audiobook)

Library of Congress Control Number: 2025924020

Cover design by Megan Elger.
Layout design by David Taylor.

12-03-2025 12:23

This book is dedicated to my wife, Elizabeth, and our four children—Daniel, Lauren, Zachary, and Luke—who lived every up and down by my side, always had my back, took arrows for me, willingly accepted more responsibilities, were mercifully forgiving, and made tremendous sacrifices to allow me to do this CEO thing.

CONTENTS

INTRODUCTION

Free up your future. Get the pink slip. Let go. Involuntary separation. De-cruit. Defund. Dehire. Deselect. De-staff. Discharge. Downsize. Indefinite idling. Make internal efficiencies. Manage down. Negotiate a departure. Reduce headcount. Reduction in force. Sacked. Dumped. Bounced. Canned. Axed. 86ed. The old heave-ho.

When my kids were little, and they heard me talking around the house about "work events" (i.e., having to fire someone, which is frequent in a life lived in significant financial turnarounds), they thought it meant poking someone with a stick that was on fire (or a torch or something more cruel) until they left the organization.

You are fired! That's the best one. But someone else on *that* reality show and in that leadership role ruined it for me (and us).

Firing is sometimes used to make an example of someone. There's nothing new about that. In the late Middle Ages in Europe, public executions served three purposes. Those in power wanted to inflict as much pain as possible on the victim while they were still alive, generate a public spectacle, and finally, deter others from committing similar crimes. In the Old West in the United States, public hangings in the town square were a form of entertainment and, at the same time, a means to deter individuals from defying laws and leaders. The same applies to discharging team members. Use the leadership tool for what it is worth. A new "sheriff" in town. Send a strong message. Meet expectations and be accountable. Or else.

The only place we don't love the metaphorical train wreck is in leadership. We don't like talking about it. We would rather put people on endless performance improvement plans or ignore the situation entirely, hoping it goes away. Even when we muster the courage to do it, we sugarcoat the departure announcement. The individual is made out to be a saint on the way out. No one knows why they left, what they did, or what line they crossed. Canning someone is the most unused and underrated tool in our leadership toolbox.

It makes complete sense that in classrooms and boardrooms, there is a hush and stillness to this dialogue. We are taught to get along when we land in school at age five. Get along with the teachers and school leadership. Get along with all our peers. Even more so today, our schools are about equality and acceptance. I value welcoming and belonging in my work. I don't value glossing over it when someone on the team is not performing and is bringing down the whole team and the organization. We don't take classes in our undergraduate and graduate education on managing and letting people go. You would be hard-pressed even to find an hour dedicated to this topic in our colleges and universities. We don't cover it in our leadership orientation when we join a new organization. Our bosses don't discuss it until the situation becomes a crisis. Even then, they try to avoid the conversation altogether or give you less than fifteen minutes to help you process the situation. I didn't land in my first "freeing up their future" dilemma with a direct report until five or six years into my leadership career. You won't either. Consequently, it was uncomfortable, cumbersome, and thorny.

If you need a good wake-up call to fully seize a powerful leadership tool, read the depressing Gallup State of the Global Workplace report.[1] In an annual survey of 160,000 of our work colleagues across the globe each year since 2009, the 2022 survey found that 60 percent of the respondents reported being disengaged at work. In the United States, half of the workers surveyed reported feeling stressed at their jobs daily, while 41 percent were worried, 22 percent were sad, and 18 percent were angry. And get this: 19 percent reported that they were miserable. Nearly one in five people we work with is either enraged, miserable, or both. According to Gallup reports, this massive shift in disengagement costs the world $8.8 trillion in lost productivity, equal to 9 percent of global gross domestic product. Jon Clifton, CEO of Gallup, says, "What can leaders do today to potentially save the world? Gallup has found one clear answer: Change the way your people are managed."[2]

The number one reason people leave their organization (when disengaged) is not about money. That is a convenient and suitable answer for the person going and a nice excuse for their leader and human resources (HR). According to surveys across all industries, money is only a factor in about 10 percent of departures. Health and family matters play a role in some situations. In a post-pandemic world, work-life balance now plays a more significant role.

People leave organizations because of their bosses, peers, or both. Their bosses aren't effective. They don't have proper team environments at work. What they have is ineffectiveness and inefficiency.

---

1 Gallup, *State of the Global Workplace* (Gallup, 2022), https://www.gallup.com/workplace/349484/state-of-the-global-workplace-2022-report.aspx.

2 Jon Clifton, "Economic Growth Is Slowing: How Should Leaders Respond?" Gallup, June 12, 2023, https://www.gallup.com/workplace/506825/economic-growth-slowing-leaders-respond.aspx.

And eventually, it turns toxic. When leaders don't take meaningful action on the dysfunction of individuals on the team and the team as a whole, their team members become disengaged, even angry and miserable. Then, they leave. The really good people go first. Not the problem children. They leave with the hope that the grass is greener elsewhere. Hopefully, they find the Oz of workplaces. What they tend to find (more often than not) is that the grass still needs to be mowed, and it turns brown if it is not watered, fertilized, and cared for. This is a leadership issue. This is about your people and your team.

How I Got Here

I was not always headed toward a career in healthcare and leadership. I didn't know what a CEO was. Being a CEO was not a career path for my family. I started volunteering at a hospital to fulfill requirements for service hours in high school. That volunteering translated into summer and winter jobs that were indoors and paid well for a college kid. I chose a college path at Notre Dame with tangible skills—aerospace engineering. In the middle of my junior year, I was stopped in the hallway by the CEO of the hospital. She was a short but caring and powerful Grey Nun, Sister Marie de Pazzi. She could tell something was wrong by the expression on my face as I walked the halls of the hospital during my patient transporter duties.

She was right. There was something wrong. I had just earned my third F. What are the mechanics of solids anyway? Sister de Pazzi pulled me into her office for a few hours. She said she was watching me and that I had the ability to succeed in healthcare. She saw leadership in me—leadership that I didn't see in myself. That afternoon, she laid out a five-year plan for me to pursue a career in healthcare leadership. Healthcare and leadership chose me. Otherwise, I would have chosen a job and career that I hated. I would have been fired. More than once. The aerospace industry is also blessed not to have me.

I've gotten really gifted at letting people go. I see it as an art. After over two decades as a CEO and operating officer, I figured it out through trial and error, with many trials and many errors. After honing my skills, I use the least-used leadership tool more effectively than most executives I know. However, you can't sharpen this critical tool until you have been let go yourself. I qualify there for a number of reasons—bankrupt company, overly political work environment, and a fish out of water on the new team, for starters. These experiences have made me better at letting people go. I learned a lot in that process, including the importance of honoring commitments, being true to yourself and the separation process, and taking just as good care of the person leaving as the new person coming on board. I also learned even more about myself, about what I wanted and needed to be happy and have fun at work. It made me a far better leader.

I was joining a new team when this book was in the works. One of the team members asked me what the book was about. I thought for over a moment and responded, "Since I am new to this group, it is best that you don't know until it has hit the presses."

Someone also asked me this question when I talked about writing this book.

"How many people have you personally fired?"

I think—I'm not quite sure—that I have personally had "the conversation" with more than fifty people. I clearly remember, in a corporate "downsizing," having to let go of fourteen people in three cities in three different time zones, in person, in one day. Turnarounds have found me in my career. Or you could say I have been attracted to the challenges of struggling organizations. It is a skill that can be developed—a rare skill in business that requires a rare personality and approach. It is akin to turning a battleship in a bathtub. So, indirectly, a couple of thousand have lost their jobs because of my leadership.

The one that taught me the most was letting go of someone who didn't report to me. The CEO called me into his office and asked me to fire a vice president–level operations leader. The senior vice president was on the road that day, and the CEO needed it done immediately that morning. I worked the office politics with my colleague and convinced the vice president to resign. I got them to leave that day. No need for severance. I was proud of what I had accomplished until I saw the CEO as he was coming back to the office and I was headed out to lunch. The CEO was irate. I was supposed to *fire* the vice president, not let them resign gracefully. He wanted to send a message to the entire organization. That public execution thing, again.

Regardless of whether you're putting someone on a waiver or facing the tip of the spear yourself, it never feels good. It isn't fun. I am not proud of it. It is what it is. I did what absolutely needed to be "done!" Inspired by his wife, Kelly Lynn, and self-described as his favorite song he has ever written, American country music singer Chris Janson had a 2019 hit of the same name that describes this book and this leadership imperative so well.

Love hits you the first time you see your soulmate—that first dance, that one kiss. You know. And you are done. Freeing up someone's future is the opposite side of the same coin as love. When you are done, you are done. There is no debate. Your head, heart, soul, and gut are all connected and headed in the same direction. When you know, you know. You are done.

This book, which is laid out as "what to look for," "how to," and "for what," will be one of your cardinal leadership tools. We will explore why we are bad at letting people go, because admitting you have a problem is the first step to solving the problem. Then, we will look at some people, personality types, and industries that are better at it. Carl Jung's twelve archetypes will be the foundation for exploring the people—the good, the bad, and the ugly—you will encounter on your team during your career. Examples from literature, history, movies, and television, along with not-so-good personal experiences from my career, will boost your comfort level with recognizing, managing, nurturing, neutralizing, and managing out the archetypes in your life. Finally, you will walk through specific steps to make it happen (and mitigate it) with grace, with your team's support, through the opposition, and with a good ending.

Finally, I want to issue a formal disclaimer. This is a leadership and business book. The stories, characters, events, and incidents are purely coincidental. Some of the names you'll see are the names of characters from one of my favorite movies! Brownie points to you if you guess which one! No identification with actual persons (living or deceased), places, organizations, companies, leaders, buildings, products, or services is intended or should be inferred. If you identify with one of the people and stories, it definitely isn't you. If you don't identify with any of the people and stories, then you have a problem because it *is* you.

Why I Wrote This Book

I am passionate about building teams. That came from healthcare and leadership picking me in that meeting with Sister de Pazzi. Being relentless about finding and developing talent. Getting the right people on the team. Ensuring that team members are grown and nurtured. Exiting team members who don't fit the culture, organization, or path forward. In teaching a short-credit course on physician alignment and engagement at Cornell University, I have encountered students in their early twenties with no management experience and mid-career entrepreneurial leaders with no formal training in business and leadership. I have seen the need from my own son, an aspiring hospitality leader, on how best to lead people and teams, navigate office politics, and manage poor performers out of the organization. This book is for you, wherever you are in your leadership journey, and wherever you want to go with leading others.

CHAPTER 1

TALENT, TEAMWORK, AND INTELLIGENCE

Talent wins games, but teamwork and intelligence win championships. –Michael Jordan

Bouncing someone isn't personal. It should never be personal. This isn't about having the most perfect people in the organization. It is about having talent, being competitive, and winning championships.

Performance Counts

A close friend who won a Super Bowl with the Denver Broncos and now does color commentary on national radio for Notre Dame football is always amazed that many organizations and leaders struggle with making the necessary personnel changes. It just isn't like that in sports. Little League, Pop Warner, high school, and college are different stories.

Professional sports is a performance-based industry. If you aren't performing, you are being traded. If you are a terror in the locker room, you are cut. If you don't put in the work at practice, you are looking for a new team. If you are being paid more than you produce, you are released. If you are a thirty-five-year-old pitcher, and there is a twenty-five-year-old with the same performance, you are replaced.

Nick Saban, head football coach at the University of Alabama, won seven college football championships (including one at Louisiana State University) and ten Southeastern Conference titles from 2003 to 2022. Saban's "The Process" has taken on a life of its own. It is his most famous phrase with reporters. It focuses entirely on the people (and their ability to focus, concentrate, put forth effort, exert toughness, and show the discipline necessary to always execute the plan.)[3] The players change every four years. The process is consistent. Winning and playing at the highest level in college football is predictable. If you don't buy into "The Process," you don't last very long at Alabama. You most likely don't get an offer in the first place.

The late George Steinbrenner was the Yankees' principal owner and managing partner for over four decades. During that time, his team won seven World Series Championships. Nicknamed "The Boss," he transformed the Bronx Bombers into baseball's foremost dictatorship and continued a championship tradition since 1923. You either love or hate Steinbrenner. There is and was no in-between.

---

3 Ranjay Gulati and Eppa Rixey, "Nick Saban: Embracing 'The Process' of Sustaining Success," Harvard Business School Case 423-033, January 2023, revised August 2023, https://www.hbs.edu/faculty/Pages/item.aspx?num=63398.

Steinbrenner once said, "Winning is the most important thing in my life, after breathing. Breathing first, winning next."[4]

He set expectations and held his teams accountable. My oldest son did a summer internship with the Yankees thirteen years after Steinbrenner died, and those standards are still firmly in place, for everyone on and off the field. He made all players cut their hair and not have facial hair. He once benched star first baseman Don Mattingly for not complying. He gave curfews to his management team. He never took vacations and worked on the Yankees 24/7/365. If you didn't meet Steinbrenner's expectations, he went to the free agent market and found someone (in most cases, more talented with better results) to replace you. At the same time, he valued the very best and paid them record-breaking salaries.

Some people seem naturally good at making people changes. Their personalities and leadership styles are built for such messy decisions. They are just wired that way.

The late Jack Welch, one of the most admired and, at the same time, most controversial leaders of the last century, believed in the twenty-seventy-ten rule of ranking workers (good, average, and poor). I am a huge fan of Welch and how he approached talent management (in terms of intentionality, performance, potential, and development). Like Saban and Steinbrenner, Welch was built for this kind of work. It wasn't rank and yank. He expected communication with those in the bottom 10 percent, telling them what was expected, telling them what to fix, and giving them plenty of runway to make progress. If that didn't work, they worked in the wrong place. People and performance

---

4 The Week Staff, "George Steinbrenner, 1930–2010," *The Week*, January 9, 2015, https://theweek.com/articles/492741/george-steinbrenner-19302010.

are directly related. During Welch's tenure as CEO, General Electric's value rose *4,000 percent.* That is not a typo.

Entrepreneurs are another set of extraordinary-minded leaders who don't typically struggle to make people changes. Entrepreneurs desire independence and resistance to authority, can be impatient, and are hyperfocused on results. Resilience is a core value of most successful entrepreneurs. They are persuasive, and they take risks. They are inspirational, motivational, and passionate and tend to work too much. Like all successful leaders, entrepreneurs are keenly self-aware and continuously work to know what they don't know. What makes them successful and willing to make the tough decisions also makes them less-than-desirable teammates. While letting someone go is gritty, for the entrepreneur, they are playing with their own money. The cost of not making a personnel change could crush the entire business. So, too, we are playing with our own money. Our paychecks (and, for some, our bonuses) pay our bills, put our kids through school, and provide us with a home, car, vacations, and retirement.

The Four Behaviors

Like the 1990s Bulls, Crimson Tide, and the Yankees, leaders need to play *big*. Research conducted over ten years as part of ghSMART's CEO Genome project found four behaviors common to CEOs who have found success by playing big.[5] You can't have all four, but you can learn and develop them.

---

5 Elena Lytkina Botelho et al., "What Sets Successful CEOs Apart," *Harvard Business Review*, May–June 2017, https://hbr.org/2017/05/what-sets-successful-ceos-apart.

Engaging for Impact

Set a direction and then engage employees and stakeholders to move forward. Think about the aviation industry, where the average profit is just $8.27 per passenger. The sector has both high fixed and variable costs; it is highly susceptible to outside events impacting demand, and we have all experienced its reputation for questionable service. That all results in a hard-earned 4 percent average net profit margin. Then, consider Southwest Airlines, which engages for impact with a deep focus on its people. Southwest aligns its people around efficiency, low-cost pricing, and innovative logistics. That is it. Only three things. That relentless alignment and focus have had the impact of forty-six consecutive years of profitability in a row. According to *Fortune* magazine, Southwest is also the eleventh most admired company in the world. Mission, people, and money at the same time … go figure.

Deciding with Speed and Conviction

A wrong decision is better than no decision at all. No decision is itself a decision. Leaders don't make great decisions all the time. I am only aware of one person who walked this earth and made entirely great decisions. He was murdered for it. Simply make all decisions earlier, faster, and with firmer conviction. Make people decisions earlier, faster, and with conviction. You will make mistakes. Don't take it personally. Make the decision and move on. The research shows that leaders with higher IQs struggle with this more than the rest. Over-thinking and over-analyzing get in the way. You will never have all the data. You will never have the entire picture colored in, especially if you are a CEO.

Jeff Bezos, who founded *that* online bookselling company in his garage in Bellevue, Washington, is famous for his practical yet unconventional and sometimes controversial advice. Oh, yeah, that online bookselling company now generates $575 billion in revenue. Bezos is well known for his customer obsession. He puts customers in front of competitors and internal dynamics, as well as customers before the bottom line. Bezos is also renowned for his decision-making, understanding two-way and one-way door decisions. For two-way doors, you pick a door, don't spend much time there, and walk out. If the decision is wrong, you go back and select the other door quickly. Some decisions are so significant that there is only a one-way door. You don't get to reverse these decisions. They are huge and costly. For these decisions, take some time, but don't waste it. Explore all your options, engage your team in the process, be careful, be deliberate, and make the decision confidently.

Adapting Proactively

There are many playbooks in business. Things that we know work all the time. Then, there are situations, such as COVID-19, where you can throw the tried-and-true out the window and start writing from scratch. There were organizations that thrived during the global pandemic. Their CEOs employed short- and long-term thinking. They leveraged their networks and scanned a wide variety of information sources. Their mindset allowed them to understand the changes earlier and, therefore, make the moves faster. While others were still pondering, they found the second door by making mistakes and adapting.

Apple's business comeback might be the most prolific turnaround and story of pivoting quickly in the last two decades. After the late Steve Jobs left the company in 1985, it struggled to the point of almost declaring bankruptcy. Jobs returned in 1997, making a series of two-way and one-way door moves. He simplified things, cut through feuds inside the organization, and micromanaged product development. Apple is at the top of its game today and is ranked eighth on the Fortune Global 500 list.

Turnarounds, such as the one Jobs pulled off at Apple, require a unique kind of leadership and a special kind of crazy. Only about one-third of corporate turnarounds succeed. You have to be an eternal optimist and, simultaneously, a practical realist. You have to be honest, calm, and direct. You must be ruthless, dogged, and disciplined yet willing to compromise and adapt. You have to be self-confident (a huge ego and an official diagnosis of narcissism help here, too), a roll-up-your-sleeves problem-solver, and more focused on results than activities.

Delivering Reliably

The ability to produce consistent and predictable results was found to be the most powerful of these four behaviors. ghSMART's CEO Genome project found that a stunning 94 percent of the strong CEO candidates analyzed scored high on consistently following through on their commitments. Leaders are paid the big bucks to follow through to deliver results.

Yet, reliable results for leaders still remain complex and elusive. More than 40 percent of companies miss Wall Street earnings expectations each quarter. QuotaPath's Compensation Trends report, reported states that 91 percent of them failed to hit sales quota expectations in 2024.[6] Miss revenue projections and you find yourself having to make onerous cost (and people) decisions. Half of the new pharmaceutical launches since 2004 missed sales expectations.

Too many leaders confuse activities with results. We are all busy. But are we busy doing the right things? Failed turnarounds, missing earnings expectations, and failing to deliver sales are all related to confusing activities with results. We can't afford to get swept away by our "to-do" lists. Don't confuse your effort and intention with results. You have to execute. Maybe (just maybe) all this has something to do with people, teams, culture, and changing out (or not) team members.

These pragmatic examples of how to drive success through talent and teamwork should be convincing enough. But then, there is the cold, hard reality that people leave leaders, not companies.

Mike Myatt, founder of N2Growth and widely regarded as "America's Top CEO Coach," wrote an article in the December 2012 issue of *Forbes* magazine about his findings from surveys in companies where he has worked.[7] Your colleagues, in most organizations, would tell you these four disturbing facts (if you took the trouble to ask them):

- More than 40 percent don't respect the person they report to.
- More than 50 percent say they have different values from their employer.

---

6 QuotaPath, *2024 Sales Compensation Plan Report: Solving the Biggest Sales Compensation Challenges* (QuotaPath, 2024), https://www.quotapath.com/resource/report-solving-biggest-compensation-challenges/.

7 Mike Myatt, "10 Reasons Your Top Talent Will Leave You," *Forbes*, December 2012, https://www.forbes.com/sites/mikemyatt/2012/12/13/10-reasons-your-top-talent-will-leave-you/.

- More than 60 percent don't feel their career goals are aligned with the plans their employers have for them.
- More than 70 percent don't feel appreciated or valued by their employer.

Organizations are simply a collection of people. People drive results. So, organizational issues are people issues. If only one cog (person, leader, team member, etc.) is performing inconsistently with expectations (whether in behaviors, tasks, metrics, attitude, strategy, or operations, among many others), they drag down the entire team. They drag down the operating unit. They can drag down the whole organization. If they report to you, they will drag you down with them. What are you going to do about it? Jim Collins, in *Good to Great*, states three simple truths for great (not just good) leadership: "But I know this much: If we get the right people on the bus, the right people in the right seats, and the wrong people off the bus, then we'll figure out how to take it someplace great."[8]

---

8 Jim Collins, *Good to Great: Why Some Companies Make the Leap ... and Others Don't* (Harper Business, 2001).

TAKEAWAYS

- Performance matters.
- Firing is the least-used management tool—to the detriment of everyone.
- You *can* learn how and when to use it.

WHAT'S NEXT

If you find yourself avoiding firing someone, you're not alone. In the next chapter, we'll look at why you're struggling.

CHAPTER 2

DISUSE, STAGNATION, AND INACTION

Iron rusts from disuse; water loses its purity from stagnation ... even so does inaction sap the vigor of the mind. –Leonardo da Vinci

Leadership can be heartbreaking. And life-threatening. After the assassination of the UnitedHealthcare CEO in New York City, companies have significantly increased security measures for their most senior executives. I have had to do the same after social media threats.

The most heartbreaking part of leadership is watching or working with a senior leader who is not ready for their role and responsibilities. They may have taken on a role that was a stretch for them at this point in their career. Or, at a more fundamental level, their skills, talents, and personality were not well aligned with those required for the role. I worked with one such executive who ascended from a middle-management individual contributor role to a most senior executive role that required strong relationship and influence skills.

In my career, I have encountered many executives stuck in this rut. This one individual was mired in tactics—not strategy—along with micromanagement, a need for power, and their inability to understand or connect with the needs of others on the team. Worse yet, they struggled with self-awareness and the ability to read the room. Hesitation, indecisiveness, and paralysis set in. This was painful to watch. It was disheartening to have to manage personally.

This misplaced manager syndrome is nothing new; it goes back to ancient times. King Arthur should never have been king. When he was only fifteen, he pulled the famous sword from the stone in a churchyard in Westminster. And, voilà! Merlin should have been king. He was a wizard, after all. He helped raise Arthur in secret as an advisor and mentor. He was known for his ability to shapeshift and make prophecies. This shouldn't be surprising, as leadership is a back-breaking profession. Leadership requires followers, and followers are cumbersome. We are especially flawed when it comes to the clumsy hiring and releasing processes.

We tend to hire too fast. HR is busy, especially trying to get on the other side of The Great Resignation (more on that in just a bit), and they are incentivized to work faster to land candidates. We skip steps along the way, such as only having the candidate talk to the recruiter. Or we don't actually meet with them several times, just once or twice. Or, worse yet, the position reports directly to us, but we get involved only at the end of the process. So many times, we don't get the opportunity to hire our team. We are stuck with them when we take the job. The board or the boss loves the team and doesn't want to see any changes. Then, you may find the team isn't really a team at all. I have inherited senior teams that have never actually met as a team. Or who thought one hour a week together made for powerful dialogue and better decisions. I landed on a team where some of the key senior executives did not report to the CEO, COO, or even another senior executive. They were left floundering and reporting to a committee of their peers.

Building a team is one of the most important things businesses must do every day. Organizations spend tremendous amounts of money and time bringing new people in, and most companies and leaders are just not really good at it. Organizations also spend tremendous amounts of time and energy trying to nurture, develop, and retain top talent. Yet, most businesses (and sports teams, for that matter, or at least the ones I follow) are even worse at that.

What Gets in the Way

The most obvious solution to ensuring you have the right talent to move your mission and vision is keeping the really good people on the team. You don't need a group of all-stars to drive performance. But you do need to attract the right talent when you have openings. And prune individuals, teams, and business units that aren't moving the ball forward. We are here to talk about the pruning part. Even the most successful leaders struggle with letting someone go. We are all human, after all, and our humanity can get in the way. Let's take a look at ourselves and what else gets in our way.

The Great Resignation: During the global pandemic, jobs became the most secure in our lifetimes. Bosses literally stopped managing people out. Employers started holding on to talent (even the most destructive talent) and hanging on for dear life. If you let someone go, there was no one to take the job or do the work (often for months, and sometimes never). The pandemic was unprecedented. This issue is conventional. We didn't let people go the way we should have before 2020 (or since, for that matter). The Great Resignation is just another poor excuse.

Desire to please others: I get that "people pleasers" are better at active listening. You build relationships much faster than others. You try hard to see things from other people's perspectives. You tend to score higher on the empathy scale. But all this gets in the way of accountability, urgency, effectiveness, and, most of all, delivering results.

If this is your core personality type, please return this book and get your money back. I have seen too many leaders (and even CEOs) with this fatal leadership flaw. You are in the wrong line of work if you are a leader who has an overwhelming desire to please others.

LEADERSHIP IS NOT A POPULARITY CONTEST.

This all sounds harsh so early in the book. Life is hard. It is not impossible; it is just plain hard. We are human and full of emotions, wants, needs, desires, and fears. We get caught in the upward pull for more and better. More and better schools, homes, food, cars, and other pleasures. We experience disease, injury, loss, grief, and death. We all have a little selfish streak in us and can be hypocrites at various times in our lives. Let's face it. We aren't always able to get along with everyone. As a cardiologist board chair once counseled me, "Your friends come and go, but your enemies accumulate." We can't escape the human condition.

So, too, leadership is meant to be tough. You have to embrace "pull leadership"—always being on (at work and in the supermarket, too), inspiring, motivating, and lifting those around you. At the same time, you have to balance "pull" with "push" leadership—prodding the team to achieve organizational goals by setting expectations, goals, targets, objectives, strategies, and metrics. You get the pleasure of navigating external forces, competitors, politics, economics, and all the shifting forces where you have little to no control. All the while juggling people, personalities, mentoring, coaching, holding others accountable, and meeting goals given to you by your boss, the board, or the market.

In all this, everyone, at some point and with some issues, avoids conflict. Yes, guilty as charged. It all stems from our innate human nature to avoid hurting others. It can be about self-preservation. Drama and trauma—at home and work—are never fun. Simple disagreements can turn epic in a heartbeat. Imagine what dismissing someone could be? Earth-shattering. Who wants that? It's better to limp along, do their work for them, have others pick up the slack, and avoid the real answer. Is it really? Avoiding conflict can also be born out of self-serving behavior. Egocentric territory. This is about avoiding personal and/or professional accountability. Let's not take action on the individual because I am up for promotion and this would look bad, or that person has a redeeming quality that benefits me (let's say at bonus time). Avoiding conflict out of concern for oneself is dangerous territory. In the process, you are hurting the other person, the team, and, worst of all, yourself.

Embracing healthy conflict is critical to your leadership, growth, and development. Embracing healthy conflict is one of the missing ingredients when building truly high-performing teams. To do this, you need to become a better and more active listener. Communicating openly, honestly, directly, and respectfully should flow from nurturing your listening skills. This is about the issue. This is about the team. This is about the organization. It is never about the person.

It is never about you. You might even need an internal or external coach (i.e., someone not in the heat of the battle at the moment) to help you think through conflicts, develop some mental models for your embrace of healthy conflict, and possibly even create some written conflict guidelines for you and your team to follow. Leverage this healthy conflict as a growth opportunity for your leadership, your team, and the organization's overall health.

Others are watching: In leadership, someone is always watching you. Are you on time? Are you engaged? Do you appear angry? What buttons should be pushed, or what subjects should one stay away from with you? Do you have others' backs? Or it could be even simpler: Is your office door open or closed? Did you engage on the elevator on the way to the car at the end of the day? How were you behaving at your child's basketball game and in the parking lot after the game? Did you even show up for your child's recital? Are you on vacation again? Another trip to Europe? The scrutiny of leadership can get really exhausting.

When making people decisions, everyone is watching you as well. Have you let someone go before? Have you let a lot of people go before? I once had my chief legal officer make a backhanded comment that he had never seen so many people on severance in a long-tenured career. Has this person been around for years? I had to let someone go, and their father and grandfather had worked their entire careers in the organization and the community. Does the person have lots of friends? Are they connected to key stakeholders inside and/or outside the organization? Will you get the reputation of being a "hatchet person"? Maybe you already have that reputation and want to work past it.

Emu Power

It is important to be self-aware and answer these questions. But you can't get paralyzed to the point of indecision. You are a leader, and you will always be criticized. It comes with the title and paycheck. All decisions will have their critics. Even the simple and easy ones. Sometimes, that criticism stings, and it can (and will) get personal. You aren't in a beauty pageant or running for office. Never ignore criticism, as there is always a grain of truth in it. Pick out the grain. Learn from it. You don't always have to respond. Sometimes, you just have to let it go. Don't play the victim. Don't hesitate. Keep moving forward.

Never surrender: One of my favorite places in the world to visit is the (Winston) Churchill War Rooms in London. To me, it represents the once reluctant leader who rose to the occasion and never backed down. Like many leaders, he had to overcome personal demons, and I admire his perseverance and resilience. One of Churchill's most famous speeches goes something like this: "We shall go on to the end, we shall fight in France, we shall fight on the seas and oceans, we shall fight with growing confidence and growing strength in the air, we shall defend our Island, whatever the cost may be, we shall fight on the beaches, we shall fight on the landing grounds, we shall fight in the fields and in the streets, we shall fight in the hills; we shall never surrender … " It was delivered shortly after British forces retreated at Dunkirk and about a month before the French surrendered to the Germans after only six weeks of resistance.

Many organizations hold governance and leadership retreats. Who "retreats" in business? In my organizations, we always advance with the board, the senior team, and other key stakeholders. Never retreat. I keep a plush emu someone once gave me on my desk as a reminder. Emus are the second-largest birds in the world, can reach speeds of thirty miles per hour, and can run great distances. Emus can't fly and can only walk forward. The emu—not just a cool commercial actor.

LEADERSHIP HAS A LOT OF THE BRAVADO OF AN EMU.

Once a manager, we want to become a director and vice president, then a senior vice president, a COO, and then, ultimately or unfortunately, a CEO. We want to top metrics in employee engagement, rock the net promoter score, have a product or service with top quality, safety, and consumer satisfaction, be the sales leader, grow/grow/grow, deliver the profitability goal, and then crush the competition. Always running forward, hard and fast. Always running the distance. Never retreat. Never surrender.

The same is true for the teams we lead. We can fix them. We just need more team meetings. We need to pull more than push. We need to step back and let them lean in. If we were only clearer with them about expectations. Put things more in writing this time around. Send more emails. We should spend more time with them. Let's find them a mentor and maybe even a professional coach. We should have high-performing team members work with them and reinforce what we have been driving toward. Throw more time, more energy, and more money at the problem.

There are times when projects, initiatives, plans, and teams require you to let go of your control. There are times with your people to surrender. Retreat. It is perfectly OK to admit to yourself (and your team and all those around you) that something isn't working, something isn't right, something is bad, something is off, and something is a waste of time. There is no need to stay on that path of frustration, loss of time, loss of money, maybe even depression, or quite possibly worse. There is no prize for the leader who has suffered the most. No bonus at the end of the year for enduring a painful team member. No victory speech on the aircraft carrier for enduring it all. The real work lies after the surrender, taking action, and moving on.

It is all your fault: You hired the person. The references were good. They earned Ivy League degrees. They worked at some of the top organizations in the industry. We lured them away from our biggest competitors. Other leaders, maybe including your boss, were supportive of the decision. You spent countless hours mentoring, developing, and nurturing them. The team really chipped in and helped you with the individual. Yet, it still isn't working. In fact, it is working miserably.

Hindsight is always twenty-twenty. It is all your fault that it isn't working. It has nothing to do with them. You put too much trust in your first impression. And the impressions of everyone else who interviewed the person. You didn't read between the lines with the references. Everyone gives and gets great references. But there are always subtle things in their words that give clues that the candidate is not so great. The person hopped around great organizations every two to three years. They didn't last beyond that anywhere. They never had to live with their decisions in the long term. I consider five to seven years a good organizational run. Maybe you were not clear about the job, the job description, or the expectations. You didn't really test for cultural fit, and they never really got into the groove of fitting in. HR didn't do or skipped the background check and/or social media scan. Or, think about it, maybe your organization is fundamentally dysfunctional for that individual, and your team and, quite possibly, you.

It is hard for people (yes, even me, and my spouse even more so) to admit they made a mistake. It is exponentially more difficult for leaders to admit a mistake, let alone say, "I am sorry." Admitting mistakes requires vulnerability. So, walk the talk. Set a positive example. Admitting mistakes furthers a culture of trust and enhances respect for you, with you, and around you. I once met Justin Bieber, and like many of his songs, his music often touches on this theme. As he once explored in song, sometimes we need to ask if it's too late to make amends. The answer in leadership? It's rarely too late if the apology is genuine. Own the mistake. Sit down with the individual whom you let down. Be honest and take personal accountability for their failure. It was really yours all along. Apologize and ensure a soft landing for the person impacted. Learn from this mistake, and don't repeat it again and again and again.

Complexities and Matrices

Organizations today are more complex than ever before. There are many rules, strategies, priorities, processes, business units, subsidiaries, divisions, partners, titles, organizational structures, decision-making apparatuses, metrics, goals, ways to get ahead, and diverse talent. There are numerous internal and external stakeholders to satisfy, along with regulators and the media (and social media). Just think about it: Walmart has 2.3 million associates, the National Health Service in the United Kingdom has 1.4 million caregivers, and Indian Railways has 1.2 million workers.

So many organizations operate in matrix structures. Initially developed for the complex aerospace industry in the 1950s, the matrix structure started to take off in the 1970s. Digital Equipment Corporation, which created groundbreaking systems such as the Programmed Data Processor and Virtual Address eXtension, became a pioneer in early software development by leveraging matrix structures. In most industries, the matrix structure was diluted by the late 1980s. In the late 1990s, my first operational director role in healthcare was a highly matrixed, service-line position. While healthcare is almost always late in adopting anything, I still love the matrix structure today, especially for engaging physicians in leadership. Nike is a famous example of a highly successful matrix structure organization. At "The Swoosh," they have functional teams such as HR, coupled with divisional teams that focus on both product and geographic region.

Whether your organization is complex, matrixed, or some other buzzword, you often find yourself reporting to multiple leaders. You even find yourself managing people who report to multiple leaders. This is done to create clearer objectives, efficiently use scarce resources, ensure more free-flowing information, and retain the workforce (especially in highly competitive markets or industries). However, things might actually move more slowly for you as a leader when you have to shuffle through multiple leader priorities, conflicts, and power struggles. When you need to make that much-needed people change, conflict, power, control, and prioritization all get in the way of reaching a decision.

While avoiding the complex and matrixed mess is a nice reason not to make a change with a team member, you need to lean into and embrace the politics of complexity. You have to adopt a collaborative approach and get all the right people (even people you don't think belong at the table for the decision) talking about the issues and problems. Play to each person's strengths. Maybe even get used to biting your tongue until it bleeds. Seek clarity and agreement about everyone's role in the process and outcome. Ensure that your relationships survive (even thrive) through this tough people decision and beyond.

HR, legal, and corporate compliance: Hiring and firing are a significant part of the role of HR and legal teams. There can be outdated practices, policies, and people in any organization. There are steps that HR might or will expect in terms of documentation, attempts at reconciliation, warnings, and avoiding discrimination. HR will need to be involved on the front end to ensure paychecks, benefits, and other items are covered and delivered after the employee's separation. Your legal counsel is there to ask questions about additional matters related to retaliation, whistleblowing, laws, regulations, employment agreements, and possibly other contractual issues. Corporate compliance might even be at the table to ensure a transition that meets internal and external regulatory, legal, internal policy, and corporate bylaw requirements.

These organizational partners in crime can be a convenient excuse for you not to take action. I've found this to be the most frequent defense. There are a lot of hoops to jump through with your advisors. There are too many decision-makers in these areas in the process of reengineering and reducing headcount. That is a good thing. It is meant to keep you and the organization out of trouble. Sometimes (or always, in the case of relieving someone of their duties), it is critical to just follow the rules.

Collaborate early and often. Collaborate effectively with HR, legal, compliance, and your communications teams when still debating the decision. Use your internal advisors to explore all alternatives, address all the issues, coordinate the process, and consider all the potential paths for action. They will be a great support for you in arranging the meeting and thinking about that crucial conversation. Together, you will craft a message for the team and organization that is clear and compassionate, as well as lay out how they will transition during this difficult change. If you doubt yourself and your ability to let someone go, remember to trust your instincts. Be an *emu*. Move ahead with your instinct. Even a wrong decision is better than no decision.

TAKEAWAYS

- This is about the organization. It isn't about the other person, and it isn't about you.
- You don't choose leadership; leadership chooses you.
- Movement is medicine in every regard, including in the workplace.

WHAT'S NEXT

Next, I'm going to give you a framework for understanding the people who work for you.

CHAPTER 3

THE FIRING ARCHETYPES

Instead of being presented with stereotypes by age, sex, color, class, or religion, children must have the opportunity to learn that within each range, some people are loathsome and some are delightful. –Margaret Mead

In social psychology, a stereotype is a belief about a particular category of people that might have an expectation about every person in that particular group. Archetypes provide guidelines for characterization, while stereotypes tend to be more limited, shallow, and typically negative. Archetypal situations or symbols are events that happen throughout our lives regardless of our backgrounds, gender, education, DNA, context, or time in history. For example, all people will experience birth, death, or a rebirth moment. Stereotyping is rarely helpful. We will be using "firing" archetypes to help us better understand ourselves, our people, and our teams.

Carl Jung, a psychiatrist and psychoanalyst who was originally a follower of Freud, is still extremely influential in the fields of psychiatry, anthropology, archaeology, literature, philosophy, psychology, and religious studies. While not formally trained, I am a fan of Jungian psychology. Sorry, Freud, Pavlov, and Maslow.

Jungian archetypes are universal symbols or patterns in the collective unconscious of all of us. They are innate and inherited, and they shape all our thoughts, feelings, and behaviors. Jung's four major archetypes look something like this:[9]

1. ***The Persona***
   Persona is how we present ourselves to the world. In the ancient world, a persona was the mask worn by an actor or actress. While this is not a lie or falsehood, how we present ourselves to the world is a fraction of the truth.

2. ***The Shadow***
   Our shadows are the ideas, weaknesses, flaws, desires, instincts, and shortcomings we keep to ourselves and hide from the world. They appear in our dreams and visions (and may take a wide variety of forms). When we are deeply angered or bothered by another person, it typically stems from seeing our shadow expressed in their persona.

3. ***The Anima/Animus***
   The anima is the feminine image in the male psyche, and the animus is the masculine image in the female psyche. Jung believed that the anima/animus represented our "true self." Adopting traditional and rigid gender roles in the face

9 Carl Gustav Jung, *The Archetypes and the Collective Unconscious* (Princeton University Press, 1980).

of this true self archetype works against us developing into our true selves.

4. ***The Self***

   This archetype represents an individual's unified conscious and unconscious. Jung often represented this as a circle, square, or mandala. In various spiritual traditions, the mandala (a geometric configuration of symbols) is employed to focus attention, serve as a spiritual guidance tool, establish a sacred space, or aid in meditation.

Since the dawn of storytelling, we have been using archetypes. We build characters, emotions, and events familiar to the human experience. It creates a sense of familiarity, connects with us deeply, and helps us easily relate to the writer, artist, or director. In literature, film, and television, we will encounter Jung's twelve archetypes and, with these examples, in very positive and affirming ways.

These archetypes also work really well in branding. Branding has little to nothing to do with names, logos, colors, and marks. What do the name Starbucks and the image of a siren have to do with coffee? The Pepsi logo was born out of patriotism during World War II, not as powerful messaging for a soft drink. Organizational branding should give your organization its identity and be informed by its identity. Questions such as "Who are you?" "Why do you matter?" and "Why do your people choose to work there?" bring your teams pride, make your organization memorable, encourage people to buy what you are selling, and deeply inform your marketing, advertising, public relations, and communications.

Your Brand

You should spend time developing your personal brand. It may seem like needless self-promotion at first. Yes, you have a great reputation. But you also need to clearly differentiate your value and what you bring to the table. Who are you? Why do you matter? Why would others want to work with, partner with, and hire you? If you work with me, read my weekly work blog, watch my videos, see my in-person messages to my coworkers in our calling, or see me speak, you will see and hear these things all the time. I hope it also comes through by the end of this book. Healthy growth—in business, in community, and in spirit. On a mission. Uprooting stagnant thinking (these are code words for moving fast and lots of change). Leading transformation. Cultivating passion into purpose. Teaching, supporting, and lifting up those around you. Helping others reach their potential to impact the world around them. A strong family commitment to social justice. Championing human dignity. Furthering the common good. Solidarity with the marginalized. That is my brand.

How can you figure out what your brand is? That's where I like to defer to Jung. Jung acknowledged that these four main archetypes can intermingle and give rise to twelve archetypal figures, also known as archetypal images. These twelve figures are the Lover, Rebel, Innocent, Everyperson, Hero, Caregiver, Explorer, Ruler, Jester, Magician, Creator, and Sage. The archetypes will fall into your lap at some point (all twelve, by the way) if your leadership career survives and thrives. We will dive deep into each of them in future chapters. The stories you will read are intended for you to connect with the archetype, not the individuals and their actions:

- *Chapter 4:* ***The Lover***
  The Lover creates intimate moments and inspires love, passion, romance, and commitment.
  Think about that good pint of Häagen-Dazs (maybe coffee or mint chocolate chip).
  Belle in *Beauty and the Beast.*
- *Chapter 5:* ***The Rebel***
  The Rebel questions authority, breaks the rules, and craves rebellion.
  Think about the branding of Harley-Davidson.
  Ferris Bueller in *Ferris Bueller's Day Off.*
- *Chapter 6:* ***The Innocent***
  The Innocent exudes happiness, goodness, optimism, safety, romance, and youth.
  Think Coca-Cola. Sorry, Pepsi!
  Dorothy in *The Wizard of Oz.*
- *Chapter 7:* ***The Everyperson***
  The Everyperson seeks connections and belonging and is known for being supportive, faithful, authentic, and practical.
  Think IKEA.
  Leslie Knope in *Parks and Recreation.*
- *Chapter 8:* ***The Hero***
  The Hero is on a mission to make the world a better place with courage, boldness, and inspiration.
  Nike and "Just Do It."
  The power of Wonder Woman and her golden lasso of truth, unbreakable silver bracelets, invisible vehicles, and razor-sharp tiara.

- *Chapter 9:* ***The Caregiver***
  The Caregiver protects and cares for others, rooted in their natural compassion, nurturing, and generosity.
  Think of eating Campbell's soup on a cold, snowy evening.
  Simple yet not-so-simple Mary Poppins.
- *Chapter 10:* ***The Explorer***
  The Explorer loves thrills, risks, discoveries, and traveling the world.
  Think of the Red Bull brand.
  Indiana Jones.
- *Chapter 11:* ***The Ruler***
  Creating from the chaos, the Ruler is typically controlling, stern, responsible, and organized.
  Think of how and why a Mercedes-Benz looks, feels, and drives better than the rest.
  Mr. Burns from *The Simpsons.*
- *Chapter 12:* ***The Jester***
  The Jester brings joy to the world through humor, fun, and irreverence, and often likes to make mischief.
  Think M&Ms.
  Steve Stifler from *American Pie* (including *2*, *Wedding*, and *Reunion*).
- *Chapter 13:* ***The Magician***
  The Magician is seen as visionary and spiritual, wishing to make dreams a reality and create something truly special.
  I love Disney for this very reason.
  And in the shadow magician or the negative expression of the archetype, Darth Vader and the iconic "Luke, I am your

father" (I love pulling that in the least opportune times with my son, Luke).

- *Chapter 14:* ***The Creator***
  The Creator is imaginative, inventive, and driven to build things of enduring meaning and value.
  Think of LEGO.
  Willy Wonka, but more Gene Wilder than Johnny Depp and Timothée Chalamet.
- *Chapter 15:* ***The Sage***
  The Sage is deeply committed to helping the world gain deeper insight and wisdom, serving as a thoughtful mentor and advisor.
  Think PBS television.
  Wax on, wax off with Mr. Miyagi.

Jung believed that understanding these archetypes would allow us to gain insight into the human psyche and better understand ourselves and others. I believe that a deep understanding of "firing archetypes" expands our possibilities to understand ourselves and our teams and take the actions necessary to better our teams, our organizations, and our communities.

So, it is only fair that I also confess what archetypes I most identify with. My primary and dominant archetype is (it shouldn't be a surprise) the Ruler. Maybe more of the reluctant Ruler, like President George Washington or Maximus from *Gladiator*. Power isn't everything. But it is very important. Important for the confidence, authority, majesty, order, discipline, stability, unwavering sense of purpose, and direction it takes to craft the agenda and translate the agenda into results. There is always a fine line between benevolent leaders and evil dictators. Even the most compassionate leader can be perceived as a villain. The world may not always agree with the path the ruler takes. Yes, enemies accumulate. Even Peter Pan becomes Captain Hook in the end.

At least three other archetypes play a less central but still very visible role in my own leadership—maybe because the Ruler is the most corruptible archetype. Maybe to avoid being overthrown. There is also the Hero with big goals, wanting to change the world, and willing to do it against all odds with stamina, courage, and more than a healthy dose of ego. The natural leadership of the hero can often turn them into a ruler, and a reluctant ruler. Plus, a little bit of the Joker (playful and disruptive) and the Innocent (humble and transparent).

Totems

Another interesting way to look at this is with totems. The West Coast First Nations—the Haida, the Nuxalk, the Kwakwaka'wakw, the Tlingit, the Tsimshian, and the Coast Salish—were most likely responsible for the first totems. My leadership teams have done a lot of work with totems. Our family has also done an exploration of totems, and we even purchased a totem in the Pacific Northwest that is featured prominently in the entry to our yard. Our totem pole features each of our six spirit animals expressing our core beliefs and values, telling our individual and clan stories, and serving as a guide and protector for our family.

My predominant animal guide—or totem, as it appears on the pole—is the giraffe. I look like a giraffe, unassuming at first, while being very tall, with a long neck and a bit of awkwardness. The symbolism of this spirit is about being centered and putting life into its proper perspective. With this totem comes a strong ability to see beyond appearances, envision the future, gently unfold an awareness about the future, and open up all the senses. There is a strong union of the force of the elements of air (curious, smart, and loyal yet fickle) and earth (firmly grounded, practical, and stable yet stubborn). There is a harmony between worldly desires and the more spiritual. The calm giraffe has an elevated spirit and the capacity to stand out from the crowd (indeed, fully enjoying standing out).

Goose Wisdom

I also have more than a little bit of goose in me. I feel connected when I see them flying overhead, lounging in my yard, or taking their time as a gaggle crossing the street, holding up traffic. Goose wisdom is about taking on quests, personally and professionally. These journeys may be true, a wild goose chase, or both simultaneously. Is the path my own or one that someone has wished upon me? The goose is kind, loyal, and brave. Family, team, community, and loyalty are intensely high priorities for them. Geese communicate clearly. They are great at setting boundaries and are aggressive at keeping them in place. Have you ever been attacked by a goose at a park? The goose, in its persona and shadow, is dedicated, determined, guiding, imaginative, imprinting, powerfully productive, protective, reliable, unwavering, resilient, self-demanding, and vigilant. Geese are not easily provoked, but don't mess with their territory.

The Team Matters Most

If you work with me or for me or have the unfortunate pleasure of managing me, you will encounter all of my archetypes and totems. I do my best work in a flock. The team is more important than the individual. We work together for the organization. Disruption, change, and transition are my things. I love accountability, and you have to love it to work successfully with me. I don't mind challenging people, teams, and the organization. I can be playful, immature, and mysterious. More often than not, this stuff works really well. But it's not all roses. I am not for everyone. Nor are you. It says nothing about me or you. When it works, it works. Other times, it just isn't a fit. It is for me, however, to figure out where I fit and who I fit with.

No One's a Total Fit

I don't fit into one archetype or totem. You don't either. It's not that simple. So, the firing archetypes don't fit neatly into just one. But it does serve as a nice way to organize, direct, and inform how you think about people and change. It is meant to increase your self-awareness as a leader and your awareness of the team dynamic. You can hear my team tell me that I am spending too much time in goose mode. Or that they need more giraffe right now to be successful. We don't choose our archetype. We don't choose our animal guide. The Ruler chose me. The giraffe and goose chose me.

CHAPTER 4

THE LOVER

I write about what I know—sex, pornography, art, fame, obsession, drugs, and alcohol. I mean, why would anyone care to listen if I wasn't an expert in what I write about? —Lady Gaga

THE LOVER

The Lover creates intimate moments and inspires love, passion, romance, and commitment.
Think about that good pint of Häagen-Dazs (maybe coffee or mint chocolate chip).
Belle in *Beauty and the Beast.*

Let's have fun right out of the gate. Sex. Drugs. Rock 'n' roll. We have all encountered true experts in these pursuits at our workplace. I have become quite the expert in this realm (not myself, just managing others). I write about what I know.

A team member emailed pornographic pictures to one of their peers to help them with a new dating relationship. Imagine having a conversation with the team members who sent and received the pictures, and both insist on having the discussion (all three of us) with the pictures as evidence. Talk about wanting to avoid the conversation before it started, let alone wanting to slide out under the door during the actual conversation. Let's just say that HR and legal were not a barrier.

Or imagine the PhD sexually harassing their direct report and claiming it was simply a cultural misunderstanding. Something got lost in translation. Or the leader having sexual relations with a direct report in the hallway. They didn't seem to notice or care that the hallways had cameras, as they couldn't make it into a room and succumbed to the heat of workplace passion.

One senior leader was in line for breakfast in the cafeteria, hiccupping and smelling like a liquor cabinet. And another senior leader was never anywhere to be found during the day because they were, unfortunately, busy managing a family member's substance abuse issues.

I almost forgot I got a midnight call that the FBI (yes, the Federal Bureau of Investigation) was staking out one of my departments. "Staking out" meant hiding in the bushes outside the building, waiting for one of my staff members to be picked up by their significant other, and then arresting them.

I am a little short on rock 'n' roll stories. There was a senior executive who was also hard to find when you needed them. But you could always find them performing with their band at local bars on weekends, during the week, and occasionally even at lunchtime. A tent card in a local restaurant that had the person's picture on it for an upcoming performance tipped me off about the transgression. You can't make this stuff up. Rock on.

Let's not leave out Me Too. If you still feel immune to this very important movement, you aren't paying attention to your team and organization. It still happens today, and it happens in your organization. There was an executive who was exploiting team members who were women, especially women whose immigration status and ability to keep working in this country were tenuous. This is where HR got in the way. Almost every team member had gone to someone in HR to report the issues in detail. The only way I found out what was really going on was an innocent question in idle chitchat outside of the bathrooms to a female colleague who was retiring shortly. She spilled the beans, and I wanted to cry. This is when you don't ask questions but take swift action. Then, you sit in front of the entire team, with the HR team members who were covering it up because they liked the executive and they were friends with them, to admit your mistake and apologize. And then, just listen to them about what you miserably failed to notice for two years.

I almost forgot the senior leader who paid for their divorce and a Cessna aircraft on expense reports. Their boss signed off on each and every expense report. The offending leader spent time in jail. Their boss skated and got a better and bigger job at another company. I've also seen a leader who paid for their child's wedding on their corporate card. Instead of addressing it, the organization chose to be less strict on everyone's personal expenses on the corporation's account. And then the silver spoon, well-heeled executive who was never in the office, never at the meetings on their calendar, always stayed in the presidential suite, had the company pay for their family's travels, and had all their personal mail delivered to the office. They sure were a great tennis partner. What were they hiding from their spouse? Inquiring minds want to know.

After all that negativity, let's briefly look at the lover in a good light. If you need more attraction, giving, receiving, nurturing, passion, devotion, bliss, and unity, search for this archetype for your team. Lovers create experiences beyond just heart, soul, and emotion that transform into a way of being. The lover in their element is personified by Gordie Lachance (played by Wil Wheaton of *Star Trek: The Next Generation* and *The Big Bang Theory* fame) in the 1986 classic *Stand by Me*. We find a mature twelve-year-old who is sensitive, introspective, and passionate. He is a natural storyteller who is open-minded, loyal, and independent, while at the same time, insecure about extensive family issues.

To build a brand on relationships and feelings, dive into the Lover archetype. This is a brand that attracts customers who are drawn to all that is premium, attractive, and alluring. This is a sphere where perception, not reality, matters the most. Practical and functional aren't nearly enough. It is a space where passion and adjective-rich word choices rule. There is a sensual feel here. The Lover loves pleasuring the senses—beautiful things, enticing smells, and indulgence—giving them and all those around joy and delight. Victoria's Secret, Hallmark, and Alfa Romeo. The red-soled shoes of Louboutin. Love, friendship, beauty, and closeness work for these premium brands. They're just not great at all for leadership. Not even for below-average leadership. Stay away from the Lover on your organizational team. It never (*never*) ends well. Run from the Lover and cut your losses expediently.

I have had the privilege of having two leaders on the team who had previous felony convictions. One served more than a year and less than five years in a federal prison. Both were extremely effective leaders. However, someone before my time missed these "small issues" when doing the background checks. It makes you think the checks were never done at all. With the second, superiors, including governance, directed the hiring, despite knowing about the conviction (stealing from the United States government, by the way), and the leader was placed in a lead organizational culture role.

This happens on a global scale more than we care to notice—to CEOs and the once-in-a-generation super talent who leave our world way too soon. The year was 1990, and the German pop group Milli Vanilli was all over the charts. They won a Grammy that same year for Best New Artist. Then, Charles Shaw, one of three singers (along with John Davis and Brad Howell) on the group's hit debut album, revealed to *New York Newsday* that Rob and Fab were fakes. They also lip-synched all of their live performances. The Milli Vanilli producer paid Shaw $150,000 to retract his statements and promptly fired him. How humiliating to hand back your Grammys and go down in history as one of rock 'n' roll's most infamous personnel realignments.

Here is another FBI story. I answered the phone one afternoon, and an FBI agent was on the other end. They asked to meet with me. I asked when, and they said they were sitting in the parking lot outside the facility. So, it was an immediate sphincter-tightening experience, and my calendar magically freed up the rest of the day. The good news was that they were not looking for me or investigating anything I may or may not have allegedly done. The bad news is that one of my leaders was securing information illegally to frame someone who was running against their family member for a mayoral position in an outlying, smaller community. Orange is not the new black.

Humans are flawed and imperfect creatures. In Roman Catholic theology, there are seven deadly sins that spur immoral behavior and other vices. These were first articulated by Pope Gregory I (the Great) in the sixth century and further refined by St. Thomas Aquinas in the thirteenth century. See, we have been dealing with bad leadership behaviors for at least 1,400 years. Maybe longer, if you consider the apple in the garden thing. Odds are that one or all of these are happening somewhere in your team. Or maybe, for your sake, it is simply sex, drugs, and rock 'n' roll.

1. *Lust*
   A strong, intense, and/or unbridled craving for sex. Think of this in the broader sense as an intense desire for anything (money, power, control, and fame are really great examples).
2. *Gluttony*
   Excessive consumption of food and drink. Drugs and alcohol would fit nicely into this vice as well.
3. *Pride*
   Excessive love of oneself and the desire to be better or more important than others. Thinking or acting in a way that suggests you are above everyone else. Think of this as the rock star disease. You can add CEOs and celebrities to this one as well.
4. *Greed*
   The desire and love for possessions. Living solely in the world of houses, cars, outfits, shoes, hats, private jets, Michelin-starred restaurants, and five-star hotels.
5. *Envy*
   The desire and love for the possessions of someone else. The sadness that results from not getting them. And the inability to rejoice in others doing well.

6. *Anger*
   Uncontrolled feelings of hate or rage. Another word for this one is wrath. So, too, this vice comes with a hunger for revenge and vengeance.

7. *Sloth*
   Just plain laziness. Also, a disinterest in the matters that matter the most—personally, professionally, in relationships, spiritually, emotionally, physically, etc.

Most of us didn't take any or enough classes to deal with any of these deeply psychological issues. OK, I might have taken six theology credits, but, admittedly, I could have been sleeping during the discussion of the seven deadly sins. I definitely know that the six undergraduate credits in philosophy and the master's degree concentration in ethics have no bearing on this chapter whatsoever. Some of us might have actually majored in sex, drugs, or rock, or all of them at the same time. Keep that to yourself.

We will dive deeper into pride, greed, envy, anger, and sloth later on in the book. While firing anyone for any reason is difficult, there are leadership orthotics and prosthetics to deal with those five and others. However, the vast majority of us are not prepared to address the sex, drugs, and rock 'n' roll issues (those deadly lust and gluttony sins). I would add not being prepared with real (not perceived or rumored) behavioral health issues to that list as well. Plain and simple. So, do your best to avoid putting yourself alone in those people situations.

According to the 2022 United States National Survey on Drug Use and Health,[10] 16.7 percent of Americans (aged twelve and older) battled a substance use disorder in the previous year, and 10.5 percent had an alcohol use disorder in the previous year. The research tells us that 22.5 percent of workers would admit that they have used alcohol and/or drugs while working. Yes, not just at home but in the work environment. The predominant substances of choice are alcohol (almost 70 percent), marijuana (24 percent), OxyContin or related products, Adderall or related products, and cocaine. Additionally, 15 percent of our coworkers admit to being high at work at least weekly. Overall, about 18.5 percent of the United States population reports having a mental health condition over the past year. There is a lack of large national studies on the prevalence of sex addiction. Still, smaller studies indicate that between 3 percent and 6 percent of the general adult population suffers from this addiction. While the suicide rate is only 0.014 percent, this averages to 132 suicides per day (the rate is 3.9 times higher in men than in women). Every year, there are more than fifty thousand assaults in the workplace, with 525 fatalities reported in 2022. Don't think your workplace doesn't mirror the statistics in the overall population. This is our reality as leaders and not something to be blind to.

---

10 Substance Abuse and Mental Health Services Administration, *National Survey on Drug Use and Health (NSDUH)* (Substance Abuse and Mental Health Services Administration, 2022), https://www.samhsa.gov/data/data-we-collect/nsduh-national-survey-drug-use-and-health/national-releases/2022#annual-national-report.

Protect Yourself and Everybody Else

Without hesitating, get your most senior and skilled HR and legal professionals with you at the table immediately. This is the realm where you have to get almost 100 percent complete information on the dynamics of the individual and the realities. There are laws and regulations unique to your community and your industry. Your organization should have policies and procedures to manage these situations. They are very often vague and open to interpretation. These situations don't always mean you shouldn't take action and remove the person from the organization. Yes, you can take action for the egregious examples above. In many situations, assuring employment (not negotiating their departure) might be the nudge they need to seek meaningful help. This is an arena where discrimination and harassment can easily take place (not just by you but by other team members who may be invisible to you). You just have to have all your ducks in a row, with all the i's dotted and t's crossed. To the extreme. Protect yourself, the organization, and the person and their family who are involved.

You are dealing with real addiction and illness. This is a medical condition, just like heart disease or diabetes. Just like most medical conditions, mental health disease is treatable. There are definitely stigmas with all this (admitting there is a problem is the first step, after all), and we are continuously expanding our understanding of how the human brain works. Treatments are available to help people who want to be helped—and who haven't crossed major lines with their behavior—to successfully manage their behavioral health condition(s). There are plenty of skilled professionals available (for those with the means and support), including psychiatrists, psychologists, advanced practice providers, nurses, therapists, social workers, and clergy. Your organization might even have a robust employee assistance program. There are hospitals and comprehensive outpatient programs where needed.

LEADERSHIP DEMANDS NOT BEING YOUR TEAM'S BEST FRIEND.

Leaders make the mistake of thinking they must be overly friendly to get things done. Results won't be achieved if your team views you as a friend and not a leader. Stop thinking you have to be friends with your team to get results. Now, ignore all that in sex, drugs, and rock 'n' roll personnel matters. These individuals dealing with real diseases need a friend, not a boss.

If one of your team members has one of these problems, they need professional help to overcome it. You are not even remotely qualified to deal with these problems. Don't think you can read books or talk to your friend, the psychologist, to manage this yourself. Giving them pats on the back, encouraging words, pamphlets on twelve-step programs, or a week's vacation to get their priorities straight are not going to do a thing.

You generally can't ask about mental and psychological disorders or conditions, emotional illnesses, or intellectual learning disabilities. Disclosure is on the individual, not you. While you know the individual needs help beyond what you and the team can provide, you can't demand that the individual seek help or make help a condition of future employment.

Work with a collaborative team of internal and external experts to manage the situation and the individual involved. You need help managing these people's issues, and the individual dealing with the problem needs help. Do your best to be a friend to get them the help they need and deserve. When the situation demands attention and action, execute flawlessly on the change and the transition.

Before your next encounter with sex, drugs, and rock 'n' roll dilemmas, ensure that your organization has clear and actionable codes of conduct, drug-free and other mental health policies and procedures, support for team members managing mental illness, training, development, and interventions for workplace violence, and paths to manage the seven deadly sins as they manifest in the office. Be sure there are educational and informational programs—maybe even a signed, all-encompassing code of conduct for employees, outlining the policies and the impact of certain behaviors.

While you were not trained in any of this, you can help yourself, and your organization should help you in being more skilled at recognizing signs of mental health, addiction, violence, and other related issues in the workplace.

TAKEAWAYS

- When firing this archetype, get professional support immediately. Do not try to do this alone.
- Shift from being the boss to being an advocate. Remember, in cases involving this archetype with a background of addiction and mental health, you will have to help them access professional resources rather than be an authoritative disciplinarian.
- Prepare your organization proactively. Ensure you have comprehensive codes of conduct, drug-free and mental health support policies, and other protocols in place right from the beginning.

WHAT'S NEXT

Take a deep breath! Next up is the Rebel.

CHAPTER 5

THE REBEL

In order to exist, [one] must rebel, but rebellion must respect the limits that it discovers in itself—limits where minds meet, and in meeting, begin to exist. —**Albert Camus**

THE REBEL

The Rebel questions authority, breaks the rules, and craves rebellion (including the organization itself). Think about the branding of Harley-Davidson. Ferris Bueller in *Ferris Bueller's Day Off.*

Leaders should encourage the Rebels and the rebel spirit in their organizations. You may call them mavericks, revolutionaries, outlaws, or nonconformists. These special people bring unique perspectives to the organization. They challenge the established norms. They take risks. They explore new and novel approaches. They are open to new ideas that can fuel breakthrough thinking and help the organization and people around them grow. They adapt quickly and keep you ahead of the competition. Their passion and conviction are contagious, in a healthy way. Their sense of purpose engages the team. If you truly embrace diversity, equity, inclusion (DEI), welcoming, and belonging as a business imperative, not just a leadership fad, you absolutely need a Rebel around you. Rebels invite psychological safety and value diverse perspectives. They are ready, willing, and able to stand against injustice and lapses in mission, values, and ethics. You can count on them to always do the right thing and make a difference for you, the company, and the world around you. Rebels challenge the status quo and will openly challenge you.

The Rebel is there to advance the growth mindset, not a fixed one. Esteemed Stanford University professor Dr. Carol S. Dweck's groundbreaking research, which bridges positive, developmental, social, and personality psychology, has implications for our educational system. Dr. Dweck wrote, "In a fixed mindset, students believe their basic abilities, their intelligence, their talents, are just fixed traits. They have a certain amount, and that's that, and then their goal becomes to look smart all the time and never look dumb. In a growth mindset, students understand that their talents and abilities can be developed through effort, good teaching, and persistence. They don't necessarily think everyone's the same or anyone can be Einstein, but they believe everyone can get smarter if they work at it."[11]

The corporate and leadership applications are solid as well. Leadership requires us to accept our mistakes as opportunities for improvement—and to recognize that these setbacks are normal and a part of the learning process—rather than look for the chance to point fingers or launch detailed investigations on what (and who) led to the mistake. This radical shift in leadership thinking offers the opportunity to embrace challenges and failures. To be more open to feedback. To see that our gifts, skills, talents, and intelligence are there to be developed. Satya Nadella, CEO of Microsoft and an advocate of the growth mindset discipline, said, "If you take two kids at school, one of them has more innate capability but is a know-it-all. The other person has less innate capability but is a learn-it-all. The learn-it-all does better than the know-it-all."[12]

What Do Rebels Look Like?

Erin Brockovich, portrayed by Julia Roberts in the 2000 film *Erin Brockovich*, was an unemployed single mother desperate to find a job. She negotiated a job with her lawyer after a failed lawsuit against a doctor following a car accident. With her earthy and rebellious nature, she investigated the shady dealings of the Pacific Gas and Electric Company. She discovered that the corporation was quietly buying

11 Carol Dweck, *Mindset: The New Psychology of Success* (Ballantine Books, 2016).

12 Chloe Berger, "Satya Nadella Transformed Microsoft's Culture During His Decade as CEO by Transforming Everyone into 'Learn-It-Alls' Instead of 'Know-It-Alls'," *Fortune*, May 2024, https://fortune.com/2024/05/20/satya-nadella-microsoft-culture-growth-mindset-learn-it-alls-know-it-alls/.

land that it had contaminated with hexavalent chromium, which was poisoning area residents. Rebel Erin found herself leading a historic class action lawsuit against a behemoth company.

The novel *The Catcher in the Rye*, published in 1951, details two days in the life of sixteen-year-old Holden Caulfield (a fictional character in the work of J. D. Salinger). After being expelled from prep school, Holden is confused and disillusioned. He begins a search for truth and rebels against the phoniness of the adult world. His rebellion extends to his first experiences with love, his thirst for freedom, and his struggle to find his identity and place. These are the things that every sixteen-year-old can identify with. We all struggle with and rebel against—at one point or another (or are still rebelling against)—alienation, losing our innocence, our world's hypocrisy (our organization's disingenuousness and grandiosity, too), fear of change, and our want and need for connectedness.

When Rebels Win

Rebels make for great CEOs under the right conditions. Courageous rule breakers are often needed to break out of the norms of the industry. One example is John Legere, former CEO of T-Mobile. Mr. Magenta, who always wears the same iconic color as the company's logo, has cultivated more than six million followers on X/Twitter. In doing this, he blurred the lines between CEO, company mascot, and digital rebel. When he joined T-Mobile, the company was one of the smallest major wireless carriers. It was failing miserably. Then, Legere almost single-handedly changed the company's fortunes. He did what his competitors would never do. While becoming the literal face of the company, he eliminated contracts, made it easy to upgrade, expanded coverage across the planet, and pushed market leadership in 5G and faster download speeds. Legere's "Un-carrier" leadership had T-Mobile crushing its competition.

Then, there is the *Rebel Without a Cause*. Consider the quintessential James Dean in the 1955 coming-of-age romantic drama about confused, suburban, and middle-class teenagers. In the movie, there is, indeed, a rebel with a cause—John "Plato" Crawford, played by the great Sal Mineo. He is an orphan who was abandoned by his divorced parents. Left in the care of his nanny, he is shy, lonely, emotionally disturbed, anguished, and desperate just to be loved. Plato's shooting at the end of the movie is a tragic and emotional end to a rebel with a cause.

Jim Stark, played by Dean, is a sensitive, vulnerable, and self-destructive teenage loner trying to make friends in a new town, find peace and a sense of belonging, have purpose in his life, and find parental guidance despite his rebellion. Smoking, drinking, and thinking his parents are tearing him apart guides his thinking and actions. If you really look at it, Jim has no reason to be a rebel. His only challenge in life is growing up. We all have to deal with that one. The rebel without a cause is simply a nuisance to himself and everyone around him.

Rebels: Pros and Cons

True rebels are charismatic and independent. They are passionate about their values and beliefs. They speak truth to power and challenge the present state of affairs. They inspire and motivate change. They are unafraid to take risks to achieve their visions. This is great for an organization. This is great for our society. The weakness of rebels is that they can become overly focused on their own agendas. This makes them completely disregard the feelings and needs of others (and their organizations). They struggle with commitment. They become disruptive and confrontational. They cause conflicts with leaders, their teams, the organization, and everyone who will engage with them. In this process of rebellion, they tend to attract partners in crime who are also looking to defy conventions. This is not good. This makes sacking them one of the easiest to deal with.

I've encountered many leaders whose rebellion shifts, at some point, from an "organizational and team cause" to "no cause" at all. Well, not exactly—it shifts to their own agendas and their own causes. This is when they get sloppy and just do things that can't be tolerated.

Some of the sloppy things are more covert. I speak from real-world experience. Like doing their own thing with their own initiatives. And telling their teams that they just don't have to do what the organization asks them to do. Disappearing when they should be leading key initiatives and covering it up along the way. Or maybe even sabotaging key initiatives through wrong direction or a complete lack of direction. Just going through the motions. Starting a search for a new job and trying to align others to go with them when they land that right opportunity (a company that values rebels, of course). They always try to align others around their rebellion, even without a cause. Fighting the establishment and stirring things up. Taking up the famous words of Ernesto "Che" Guevara (the Argentinian physician, revolutionary, and guerrilla leader), "We cannot be sure of having something to live for unless we are willing to die for it."[13]

---

13 "Ernesto 'Che' Guevara Quotes," QuotesData.com, accessed September 26, 2025, https://quotesdata.com/Ernesto_Guevara.html.

Rebels Behaving Badly

If you ask the right questions and listen intently, the sloppiness will become overt, deliberate, and intentional. Essentially, they are daring you to do something about their revolution:

1. Late, being sick, and taking ill-timed vacations, notably missing essential meetings in which they have to lead the team
2. Open refusal to follow instructions and guidance, which is typically coupled with a publicly disagreeable and even aggressive tone and language
3. Threatening behavior and words, not of the violent kind but of the "do this or else" genre, which may also grow into bullying and other aggressive behaviors
4. Previously good performers not accomplishing even the smallest tasks
5. Sharing confidential and proprietary information (including discussions from team meetings) with anyone they can find who will listen
6. Using company resources (including people) for personal endeavors
7. Lapses in veracity, false statements, fudging facts for personal gain, cover-ups, and blatant lying

The story of Colonel Claus von Stauffenberg, played by Tom Cruise in the 2008 movie *Valkyrie*, clearly illustrates how this works. Tom Cruise always plays the Hero, but, from another perspective, his character is every bit the Rebel in this classic. Colonel von

Stauffenberg serves Germany with extreme loyalty and pride, but he deeply disapproves of the grossly terrible things being perpetrated. That brings him to the realization that his beloved country will be destroyed if the Nazi forces are not stopped. He joins a group intended to overthrow the leader and takes the key role in the assassination. After the coup d'état fails, von Stauffenberg takes a bullet in the shoulder in a brief battle that ensues. He and his three closest colleagues are overpowered and immediately taken into the Bendlerstraße's courtyard to be shot by the firing squad. The Colonel's last words are, "Long live our sacred Germany!"

Shortly after the movie was released, a close friend asked me what the only lesson I should take from *Valkyrie* was. I was engaged in some Rebel behavior in my first CEO job (with a cause but not the organization's cause). All these years later, I remember what he said and how he said it clearly: "If you are going to kill the king, *kill* the king!"

If your organizational Rebel gets to the point of killing the king, the team will stop them from finishing the act unless you are a despicable dictator. Then, they will join the cause. Most of the time, they will come directly to you (not just one or two team members but many, and as a team) to make a change immediately. Even those on your team who sprint in the opposite direction of conflict will become enraged and demand action—in private with you and the team, but also in public settings in front of the Rebel and their army. Rebels damage relationships to the point of no return. For the Rebel, resistance (and not the good kind) is as natural as breathing. However, their personal compass (their true north) never fully develops. When the stakes become high, their self-awareness is questionable and often practically nonexistent. They start to confuse what they want, what they believe in, and who they really are. This leads to pushing boundaries to the point where it becomes all about proving others wrong.

They visibly overreact to all situations. They launch major team and organizational power struggles, which escalate to tearing down everyone and everything in their path. Chaos and havoc follow them wherever they go. Complete and utter destruction lie in their wake.

How to Manage the Rebel

Rebels serve an important purpose in companies. The team rallies around them because they, too, desire change as well as challenge injustice and oppression. But, at some point, they only represent the fringe with a blatant disregard for consequences. The Rebel always craves attention, and the team will eventually (almost always) grow tired and demand swift and immediate action. Teams don't like destruction. Especially when they are the ones stuck with cleaning up the mess. When it gets to that point, there is no choice but to remove the leader quickly. This story has played out since the beginning of time. From King Xerxes I of Persia in 465 BC to Emperor Julius Caesar and the Ides of March, to Lady Jane Grey in 1553, to King Charles I (and the second King Charles) in 1649. Even modern-day Rebel rulers, such as Muammar al-Qaddafi in Libya, Samuel Doe of Liberia, and Maurice Bishop in Grenada, seized power violently and faced the exact same fate. After years of torturing their own people, some of the most ruthless Rebel archetypes, including Iraqi dictator Saddam Hussein and Afghan leader Mohammad Najibullah, were executed by their own people.

Organizations need a little rebellion when times call for being more creative, dynamic, fun, and even wild. In times when the organization is static and stuck, or, at the very least, needs to look at different ways of thinking and reconsider tried-and-true views. When you want to be far more mission- and values-focused. When you need more passion and energy. When you are searching for abundance, attraction, and an openness to all the possibilities.

You don't always need a Rebel on your team. Don't make the mistake that it is always cool to have troublemakers, guerrillas, free spirits, misfits, and outlaws in the room. Sometimes, you don't want to impose minority views by force. Or you don't need to free the organization from the leadership and/or direction of the past. There are times in your leadership path when complaining, a "me versus we" focus, pessimism, alienation, problems (that are vocalized), worrying, pointing fingers, and lecturing aren't even remotely helpful. Sometimes, you, your team, and the company as a whole crave stability. Demand direction and control, and push leadership to get where they absolutely need to go to survive and thrive. William Shakespeare's line from *Henry IV, Part 2*, sums up the fate of the rebel without a cause and your role as a leader in managing people: "Uneasy lies the head that wears a crown."

TAKEAWAYS

- Recognize the escalation pattern. Rebels tend to follow a predictable path, starting with passive-aggressive behavior and progressing to openly defiant acts.
- Always monitor team dynamics. Rebels tend to have the support of the teams they work with. Take action when you feel they have begun to alienate the team.
- Assess when rebellion is useful versus destructive. Rebels are useful when organizations need creativity, energy, and fresh thinking. It is up to you, as the leader, to decide when to take what action.

WHAT'S NEXT

Next come the folks who are simply in the wrong place at the wrong time—the Innocents.

CHAPTER 6

THE INNOCENT

I think people who go out and tell you how much they're gonna change things are the people who end up being just another whatever. I'm never trying to change anything. That's not for me. **–Darius Rucker**

THE INNOCENT

The Innocent exudes happiness, goodness, optimism, safety, romance, and youth.
Think Coca-Cola.
Dorothy in *The Wizard of Oz.*

The number of mergers and acquisitions (M&A) in the United States has fluctuated significantly in recent years. In 2021, there were almost twenty-five thousand M&A deals. In 2022, the volume decreased to just below twenty-one thousand. In 2023, we saw the lowest number of transactions in the past five years globally. However, one-third of the Standard and Poor's (S&P) 500 company growth comes directly from M&A activity.[14] Frequent acquirers across all industries have been shown to generate increased value (in the publicly traded arena) and increased shareholder returns.

Historically, M&A deals have resulted in significant job losses. If there are job increases after a significant M&A transaction, you are likely doing something wrong—the worst kind of wrong you can think of. If you are not reducing costs significantly in M&A, including and especially people, then you are not delivering on value and returns. You just don't need duplicative information technology shops: one digital and social media team, not two. You don't need two chief financial officers (CFOs). I worked in an organization where we ended up with not two but four CFOs after a merger. Imagine those meetings and the four different monthly financial reports. Who's on first?

Around 30 percent of all positions, regardless of the industry, are deemed redundant in a merger process, and even more in a larger corporate acquisition. Don't believe in the "merger of equals" messaging; there is always one of the two parties that assumes control—call them the "winner." If you are a leader in a company that is merging, you should feel anxious and worried about your current and future job prospects, especially if you sit in the "loser" organization. If your organization is being acquired, brush up your resume,

---

14 S&P Global Market Intelligence, *Global M&A by the Numbers: 2022 in Review* (S&P Global Market Intelligence, 2022), https://www.spglobal.com/market-intelligence/en/news-insights/research/global-ma-by-the-numbers-2022-in-review.

start engaging your career network, and get those executive search consultants on speed dial.

Since 1970, there have been at least seven recessions in the United States. The 1990s were the longest period of economic growth in the history of the United States to that time. The dot-com bubble bursting and the September 11 attacks brought on a recession that started in March 2001 and lasted for eight months. Job losses totaled $1.6 million, or 1.2 percent of the prerecession level of employment. The Great Recession, which lasted for eighteen months from 2007 to 2009, was initiated by a burst in the housing bubble. Many of our tried-and-true financial institutions, as well as the auto industry, failed or collapsed. During this time, an average of seven hundred thousand workers lost their jobs per month.[15]

Corporate layoffs are simply a cost-cutting measure—typically impacting groups of workers rather than just one or two people here and there. Nothing more and nothing less. I had a CEO boss who insisted that layoffs were the product of failed leadership. Layoffs are an exceptionally effective strategy to turn the tide in short order. The environment is rapidly changing, so strategy and financial performance must also change rapidly (preferably proactively). Over 15 million people were laid off in 2022 (about 4.8 percent of the total working-age population in one year).[16] Post-pandemic trends—coupled with weak consumer demand and surging inflation—are impacting the need (let's call that a leadership imperative) to downsize the workforce.

---

15 Christopher J. Goodman and Steven M. Mance, "Employment Loss and the 2007–09 Recession: An Overview," *Monthly Labor Review* 134, no. 4 (April 2011): 3-12, https://www.bls.gov/opub/mlr/2011/04/art1full.pdf.

16 Greg Iacurci, "2022 Was the 'Real Year of the Great Resignation,' Says Economist," CNBC, February 1, 2023, https://www.cnbc.com/2023/02/01/why-2022-was-the-real-year-of-the-great-resignation.html.

Corporate layoffs are a standard business practice. In 2023, almost 60 percent of *Fortune* 100 companies had some form of layoffs. They were once a rare event for organizations facing bankruptcy, acquisition, or closure. It's the era of short-term performance expectations and doing more with less. I think too many CEOs—I plead guilty here—overly rely on layoff plans to fix more fundamental issues. When the rest of the environment seems out of control, costs and people cuts are controllable. Layoffs are an "easy button." If you surveyed CEOs right now, over 80 percent of them have plans for significant cost cutting and layoffs. How many actually achieve them? In reality, very few follow through. A lot of talk with very little action. Bragging about being tough and taking out $100 million in costs last year. Good luck finding it on the bottom line. Like avoiding de-staffing underperformers, most CEOs and senior leaders shy away from the tough decisions of cost cutting and headcount reductions. We can just grow revenue and volume and sell more and market more. That will fix the gap—not!

I don't suffer from that affliction. It's not a gift, but it is something I have become really great at, and I have been fortunate to have bosses and mentors who have taught me and helped me refine my skills along the way. I don't like doing cost work. I don't like layoffs and cutting people. I just keep finding myself taking on that role and landing in those organizational situations, and most of the time, it is not my own doing.

The Innocent are merely victims of this organizational reality. You will regret these moves—well, most of them—for the rest of your career and into your retirement. There is one that still sticks with me to this day. I have never remedied the "mistake" (for various reasons, and I doubt I will ever have the opportunity), although I take comfort in the fact that my spouse is still connected to them, their spouse, and their family two decades later.

I promoted this individual early during my tenure in my first CEO role. Let's call them Stu. They had everything you needed to change performance and build a high-performing team. Stu was always positive, understood their role, respected others, supported their team members, solved problems, and delivered results (without question or worry). Stu lived the mission and values, listened, spoke truth to power, encouraged feedback, and celebrated successes. Stu was an up-and-comer with unlimited upside potential who had already mastered ensuring performance. Stu rapidly gained momentum in their new and expanded responsibilities. Sounds too good to be true? It was true. Then, financial realities hit. We were losing far more money than we thought (that CFO has a chapter later in the book). Our revenue base couldn't support our cost structure. We couldn't support the operating model (specifically, a robust matrixed service-line structure) that our original strategy distinctly demanded. This individual was leading an area that fell off our adapted plan and new priorities. Stu got caught up in the mess. Really, really good people get caught up in these messes. If there is a happy ending in all this, this individual is a CEO in their own right today (both earned and deserved).

Firing the Innocent

I like to credit my German American mother, who grew up on a farm in northwestern Ohio, for giving me the DNA and developing my personality before the age of five, for having that special sort of "crazy" to do this work and do it well. You have to be a problem-solver and self-confident with the ability to embrace conflict, engage a tight inner circle, and deal with detractors, resistors, the back channel, and pushback. It is important to be absolutely clear about expectations, roles, responsibilities, and decision-making while holding that veto authority as the "big boss" tightly. Drive toward results—not toward confusing activities for moving the ball forward—by motivating, supporting, and influencing others. You don't have to have the stereotypical German inflexibility, obsession with rules and order, use of defense as the best offense, lack of friendliness, directness, seriousness, and lack of humor. Or the stereotypical farmer personality—perseverant, passionate, committed, adaptable, and relentless about quality. But if the shoe fits, as it does in my case, own it.

Sometimes, Even SpongeBob SquarePants Has to Go

SpongeBob SquarePants (in the cartoon of the same name that launched in 1999) is the eternal optimist. The innocent and happy-go-lucky yellow sea sponge who lives in a pineapple under the sea. Full of energy, love, and excitement. At the same time, he is hyperactive, childish, clueless, and accident-prone. Don't get lost in all this. SpongeBob is the most powerful character on the show. He is very determined and never gives up, despite the odds. You will find that he is able to outsmart his opponents (especially Mr. Krabs and Squidward) and always manages to find a way to win (and win-win). He teaches us that friendship is everything. Everyone needs help at some point. Always have fun like a child. Love your work. Just be yourself.

You are, undoubtedly, going to have to fire someone you don't want to, someone you care deeply about. You will have to fire your

SpongeBob. You know, in your heart and soul, that it is a bad decision for the individual and you, but this isn't about them or you. This is about the future of your organization. We have already covered what happens to you when your company fails and gets acquired by a corporate giant or is the "loser" in a merger of "equals." Be firm. Cut to the chase without any small talk or excessive talking. You know them, and they know you. You both know that this sucks. Be fair.

Being unemployed is not good. I've been there. Finding a job is easier when you have a job. If you don't have a job, six to nine months is perfectly acceptable to find a new job (beyond that, it could become a problem for new employers). In a deeper sense, unemployment messes with who you are at your core. Losing a job impacts a person's career, self-image, and, most of all, their financial situation. This may not be as big a deal as you might think at the time, but you can't help but make it a huge deal. According to research, workers who have been laid off suffer from anxiety and depression at twice the rate of the average worker. You should absolutely support the Innocent with resources in their job search, such as formal outplacement services, offering to serve as a reference, and connecting them to your network of potential new employers.

What If You Are an Innocent Who Got Fired?

Being laid off impacts family and relationships. It completely disrupts norms and dynamics. You used to be at work all day, and now you are not. Other family members may need to seek employment to fill financial gaps caused by your change. When you're looking for a job, you can be picky about the role or location, but not both. As you seek new employment consistent with where you were and where you see yourself, it may very well mean moving. If you have children, that new city means a new home, a new room, a new school, new friends, and tryouts for sports and activities. It is even rougher if you have a child in the middle of high school. We didn't realize this until our daughter wrote her college application essays about how bad going to three high schools in four years really was. Guess who got all the blame? Now, don't feel so bad for her because she went to Notre Dame and then medical school right after earning her bachelor's degree. Things aren't really that bad. However, they were to her at the time.

What Happens After the Firing?

This serves as a caution to consider the individual, their family, and their broader relationships when thinking about the support you and the remaining team provide after a layoff. When the organization shrank, you were one of the lucky ones. You had to let some great talent leave the organization. You and others who are sticking around get to watch them clean out their offices, help walk them out of the building for the last time, and go to "going-away" parties. I love how this all works at Bloomberg, the $10 billion financial, software, data, and media company founded in 1981 by Michael Bloomberg (the former mayor of New York City). No parties when you leave. No coming back ever if you voluntarily leave the company.

The range of emotions you feel as a survivor after a big layoff is very real. You have to manage your workload effectively. The people who left were very busy (hopefully focused on results, not activities).

Who is going to pick up the slack? Manage all expectations about what happened, why it happened, what it means for the organization, and what is going to happen going forward. Communicate more than you think you should. This is a time for more one-on-one and team meetings. Give the space and time for the team to process the changes (on their own, with you, and as a team). And never ever say that "this was it." It's not the last one. Cutting costs and cutting people are our business reality today and for the foreseeable future.

TAKEAWAYS

- Separate personal feelings from business realities.
- Provide support during transition.
- Manage the aftermath with the team that survives layoffs.

WHAT'S NEXT

Next, we will look at the Everyperson—supportive and faithful, but not immune to firing.

CHAPTER 7

THE EVERYPERSON

The upward course of a nation's history is due in the long run to the soundness of heart of its average men and women. –Queen Elizabeth II

THE EVERYPERSON

Seeks connections and belonging and is known for being supportive, faithful, authentic, and practical.
Think IKEA.
Leslie Knope in *Parks and Recreation*.

Douglas Adams started with a BBC radio series that morphed into *The Hitchhiker's Guide to the Galaxy*. In the novels, TV shows, and movies, we follow Arthur Dent, the completely average protagonist. His house is about to be demolished to make way for a new road. Then, the Earth itself is about to be demolished to make way for a new intergalactic road. Ford Prefect, Arthur's friend and the undercover alien and contributor to the interstellar travel guide, helps Dent escape. This zips Arthur around the galaxy on a wacky, surreal adventure.[17]

I first read the book in my freshman year in high school, just two years after it was published. What fourteen-year-old doesn't identify with Arthur Dent? What person of any age doesn't strongly identify as well? Beyond escaping from Earth and being a space traveler, Arthur has a perfectly ordinary middle-class life. With ordinary ideas. Passive, befuddled, and bumbling. The universe doesn't make any sense to him. Yet, the dangers always make sense. Dent is not the typical hero. None of us is. He is a fish out of water. That was me at fourteen. That is me now. Then, dressed in only pajamas, he is thrust into an unfamiliar world, traveling the universe and making weird and wonderful friends. That is leadership. That is what it feels like to be a CEO. It's weird yet wonderful.

A little closer to home, Jim Halpert from *The Office* is a regular guy we can easily identify with. He lacks direction and isn't looking for it. Yet, he wants a place where he belongs and to be part of a group of people where he feels welcome. He finds just that at Dunder Mifflin's Scranton office. It is a workplace (selling paper, of all things) where he can pass the time with antics that make his life and the lives of those around him a little less miserable. He can be condescending, smug, arrogant, immature, and a know-it-all. And no one cares or notices.

---

17 Douglas Adams, *The Hitchhiker's Guide to the Galaxy* (Harmony Books, 1980).

We all have a bit of Jim in us and wish we could express it a bit more. But Jim, the Everyperson, at his core, is an affectionate, charming, funny, kind, mild-mannered guy who finds his soulmate sitting right near him the entire time.

My first CEO job was in the Natural State of Arkansas. Oh, wait, the Walmart state. "Save Money. Live Better." The company was founded in 1945 by a former JCPenney employee on a crusade for the Everyperson. Low prices to earn higher volumes at a lower operating margin. After eight decades, the low-margin proposition is the largest company in the world, with more than $600 billion in revenue and an operating margin of $60 billion. Create value by offering low costs and being inclusive rather than focusing on a targeted group. Connect with the customer by putting yourself on an equal footing with them. Pioneers who put almost every product imaginable under one roof. Products that value regular and uncomplicated things in life. I did the first "Clinic at Walmart" deal in the country with Walmart. I also executed the largest healthcare partnership deal in NFL history when the family acquired the Denver Broncos. The Denver Broncos are the real deal—sincerity, common sense, and hard work.

On the first day of that CEO job, my new boss called to tell me he was taking another senior position within the larger corporation. And he would be doing a search for my new boss. On my second day on the job, I met with the board executive committee, and they told me I needed to "clean house" with the senior team. Every single person. Had they mentioned that once in the five-month interview process? Day three—Wednesday (hump day)—was unremarkable in hindsight. Day four produced a certified letter from the National Labor Relations Board (NLRB) stating that we were going to have a union vote. In the letter, the NLRB set the vote for my fortieth birthday. Happy birthday!

The individual leading our efforts to avoid unionization (the vote finished at midnight on my birthday, and we lost miserably) was the Everyperson. It became readily apparent within one month of the two-month adventure. In those first thirty days, I had to sit down with the board and my corporate leaders to share, in a painfully blunt way, that we were going to lose the union vote and that we had major leadership issues. Not as pervasive as believed on day two, but still requiring significant action. This particular leader was humble, compassionate, and kind. I connected with them. Everyone in the organization was deeply attracted (in a personal sense) to them. They were a regular leader. Doing regular leadership things. Nothing extraordinary, but still charming. However, this new set of circumstances (a new CEO and a lost union vote) confused them. They didn't adjust. They didn't know how or what to adjust. They couldn't read the tea leaves. The pressing need to survive, thrive, move forward, and grow was puzzling to them.

Another executive on that team fit the very same profile. Let's call them Jade. Jade was hardworking. Harder working than anyone else on the team (present company included). They generated a ton of work product and activity. The first in the parking lot in the morning and the last one out well into the darkness every single day. They were authentic and wholesome. They had worked their way up in the organization over the course of more than two decades. They were friendly, humble, sincere, and a team player with a complete lack of pretense. Jade would knock down a wall or take a bullet for me and everyone on the team. There was one problem. They couldn't identify the wall that needed to be taken down. They wouldn't suspect a bullet was headed someone's way. Jade had to be told. And directed about the wall and the bullet.

When you dare take down the Everyperson, their supporters will come out of the woodwork. Not in the way that supports you making a change, by the way. Yes, *everyone* identifies with the Everyperson. They are empathetic. Why aren't you? They are humble. Why aren't you? They work hard. Harder than you. They are kind. Why aren't you? They are easily satisfied. Why aren't you? They are honest and stand for equality. Taking them out seems dishonest. And just not fair. No one wants the Everyperson to pay that price. I made some career-long enemies by removing the two Everyperson leaders above at the ninety-day mark of my first CEO role. Just imagine killing Arthur Dent at the end of the book or closing the local Walmart in Arkansas.

In my second CEO role, everyone knew the Everyperson was not hitting the mark and needed to be changed. I was their peer for several years before promotion and knew things weren't going well. It was a puzzlingly obvious situation. No one wanted to do anything about it. As a peer, they were easygoing, always willing to listen, heart-warming, neighborly, and consistently helpful. They were fun. I found them practical, friendly, approachable, supportive, and sturdy. I got promoted to be their boss, and none of this changed. In fact, one could even say all of these attractive qualities were magnified. They were my greatest champion.

When I met with the "big" CEO and COO for the first time in this new role, I asked, "If you were in my role, what would be the first two to three things you would do?" I always ask this question when taking on a new role (of every person in the organization). It is important to ask far more questions (like in a ten-to-one ratio) than make statements when assuming a new leadership role. Yes, listening matters. Both of their answers were the same. They would only do one thing. They would fire the individual I am talking about here. Both of them would have fired the individual a year or two ago. Why hadn't they done it? Why were they now demanding that I do it? There had been numerous key stakeholder issues worthy of attention over the previous two years. But, in reading the individual's recent annual performance assessment (completed right before I took over as their boss), they had a glowing review. Had all the issues gone away? Well, at least, none of them were mentioned anywhere in the review. In fact, they received a better review than I did, and a heartier raise as well. I got promoted (they weren't even considered for the role), and now I got to deselect them. Surprise!

I sat on taking action on this one for a good six months. Yes, procrastination. Yes, I was close to them. It didn't make any sense to me. However, this individual made a crucial mistake that led to their own demise. They wanted me to interview a key stakeholder group and get overly involved in what I thought was their domain. Begrudgingly, I set aside two days to travel to their market, meet with fifteen key stakeholders (individuals and groups that drove *all* of their market revenue), and dip my toes into their areas of responsibility. Not recommended for leaders, but I was stuck. By the third interview, everything was crystal clear. Each of the key stakeholders was ready to take action on their own. Any one of those contemplated actions would have been devastating to the short- and long-term reputation of the organization and its future. If someone (that meant me) didn't take action immediately, they would walk. They would take all the business to competitors without hesitation. The last of the fifteen key stakeholders sat in a governance role. I didn't ask them any questions. I needed to deliver the message that I had heard them and that I would be taking action. I would extend my visit to make it happen and manage the consequences of the change.

I sat down with key board members right after all the interviews were completed. That last stakeholder (and two others I had interviewed over the previous forty-eight hours) was in that room. I laid out the issues factually. There was a lot of tense and direct dialogue that went around the room well into the evening. That kind of disagreement with respect is good for creating high-performing teams. It is critical for good governance. It is sorely needed in our country and our country's politics. The three stakeholders supported the dialogue and path forward. We got unanimous agreement on what needed to be proposed to a full board meeting the next day at lunch.

I spent the next morning on the phone, ensuring I had agreement all around before lunch. The "big" CEO and COO were briefed on what I had found and the plan for moving forward cleanly. The three stakeholders and I initiated the conversation over sandwiches and salad. Although there had been an apparent agreement the day before and that morning, the board bailed on the decision. They didn't want to take action. We had never had such a genuinely authentic leader. What would the community think? How would we explain getting rid of a leader everyone loved? Everyone loved their entire family. Had we made a mistake in hiring the person? Could we take more time to try to fix this and them? Surely, there was another solution?

It was a little too late to find out that we had agreed on something where we didn't have an agreement. I missed some of the assumptions along the way and ended up disappointing everyone in the room on both sides. This is what we call a shallow agreement. Where I did have deep agreement, the three key stakeholders of the broader group stood their ground. They threatened to take all their business to a competitor. They rationally laid out all the reasons. They weren't personal. It was about business, the organization, and the community. Well past dessert and coffee, we got to a unanimous vote. I met with the leader right after that vote and was clear and direct about the issues and the actions. It all went well.

I woke up the next morning and was surprised yet again. It had all gone well, right? Sort of. The team was on board with the decision. Their leader was flawed, and they all knew it. The leader lacked ambition and drive, and they all knew it. It was impacting them. Their teams. The organization. Their customers. They were hearing about it in the supermarket. They wanted more and better. They were ready to move. The key stakeholders (yes, the people who drove the entire top line) were ecstatic. This was the change they were looking for. Why had it taken so long? So happy, Peter, that you finally took action. Unanimous vote? Not quite. Right there in the next day's newspaper was the board chair being quoted as having no idea why their CEO had been fired. Yes, they had been in the meeting. They had called for the vote.

Firing the Everyperson

When you negotiate a departure like this, those around you and the decision (even being intimately involved in it) will bail on you. This isn't hypothetical. It happens all the time with an Everyperson departure. You are getting rid of Peter Parker, the friendly neighborhood Spider-Man. This type of undermining isn't personal or meant to be destructive. No one wants to be the Green Goblin to Peter Parker or Dwight Schrute to Jim Halpert. This undermining does impact you, your leadership, the teams, and the organization. You can't let it go. You have to manage it. It happens with this big decision, and then it happens with more significant decisions. When the board does it, everyone can do it. Rifts, conflict, and toxicity become the norm (if they haven't already before this).

The most effective way to manage this is in how and who you hire to replace the leader you just dismissed. With that board, finding the right new leader took a good year (with me serving in the role in the interim). We spent much time and energy wrestling with (not surprisingly) more Everyperson archetypes. More kind and affable than the previous kind and affable. You don't always need to hire a superstar. You don't need all superstars on your team to be successful. Ask the Los Angeles Lakers and Brooklyn Nets superteams in the NBA.

You do need a particular bright "star" to replace an Everyperson. They need to have a set of specialized skills. An expert in certain domains is important for that business at that time. Someone with depth and breadth. They need to be able to balance both leading with power and leading with influence (with an emphasis on influence). You want a confident leader who is always overprepared, optimistic, and able to pivot in even the most difficult situations. This is a place where your instinct and interview prowess alone aren't going to get you there. More on hiring slowly and hiring right later in the book.

I took a new CEO role a year after this story fully unraveled and the Everyperson's replacement launched. We took our time and found a seasoned leader (who was coming back to the company) who was secure in their own shoes. A year into having that new CEO, I received a text from a number I didn't recognize. One of their board members (the vice chair) bailed on me and our decision (not so publicly as being quoted in the newspaper, but I am convinced loudly at the country club that weekend). The Vice chair thanked me for the decision. What? It was the best decision, although they had vehemently disagreed with it at the time. The organization was now thriving. The key stakeholders who drove the change were highly engaged. The board was in the right place and governing effectively.

The customers were delighted. The team was happy and producing results. Everything was on the upswing after the Everyperson.

We do need the Everyperson in our organizations and more of what they bring to the table. We need more humility, authenticity, and honesty. We need a greater sense of welcoming, belonging, and inclusivity. We need a sense of community, team, and maybe even family. It is the ordinary and hardworking employees who do the real dirty work. But as we just saw, sometimes even the Everyperson needs to be exited.

TAKEAWAYS

- Expect and prepare for internal undermining and a chain reaction of toxicity and rift within the organization, which will have to be actively managed.
- Replace the Everyperson with a different kind of leader.
- Recognize that it will take time for the decision to be processed.

WHAT'S NEXT

Next, we're going to look at the Hero. What could go wrong?

CHAPTER 8

THE HERO

How am I supposed to prove myself if nobody will give me the chance? –Hercules (from the Disney movie of the same name)

THE HERO

The Hero is on a mission to make the world a better place with courage, boldness, and inspiration.
Nike and "Just Do It."
The power of Wonder Woman and her golden lasso of truth, unbreakable silver bracelets, invisible vehicles, and razor-sharp tiara.

We define ourselves and our ideals by our heroes. We yearn for courage, honor, and justice. In the immortal words of Colonel Nathan Jessup (played by the acclaimed Jack Nicholson) in *A Few Good Men* (1992), "We use words like honor, code, loyalty. We use these words as the backbone of a life spent defending something. You use them as a punchline. I have neither the time nor the inclination to explain myself to a man who rises and sleeps under the blanket of the very freedom that I provide and then questions how I provide it! I would rather you just said, 'thank you' and went on your way; otherwise, I suggest you pick up a weapon and stand a post. Either way, I don't give a ____ what you think you are entitled to!" Heroes—even Colonel Jessup—are on a mission to save the world. Who doesn't need saving?

We need Odysseus, king of Ithaca, from Homer's *Iliad* and *Odyssey*. I hated those books in high school (and get a queasy feeling now writing about them). What does the tall, attractive, and most well known of the early Greek heroes have to do with a thin, pimply kid looking to get out of New Jersey? He crafted the plan to infiltrate the city of Troy using a giant hollow horse and personally led the siege. In his victory, the army desecrated temples and the altars of the gods. That didn't sit well with the gods. On his journey back home to Ithaca, the gods laid a fierce storm, scattering his army. We then follow him on his far-out ten-year struggle to get back home. Odysseus is sharp, intelligent, resourceful, curious, and cunning. He is noble, strong, and courageous, with a thirst for glory. Odysseus is consistently loyal to his wife, army, and kingdom, no matter the challenge. He is willing to make any sacrifice for what he truly loves.

I need *Rudy*. Yes, that Rudy Ruettiger. He makes more sense to me than Homer. Rudy lives and breathes Notre Dame football. Going to Our Lady's University is a pipe dream, but Rudy is optimistic and relentless—downright Pollyanna. He keeps going when everyone around him tells him what he seeks is impossible. Even his father offers advice to play it safe and not be a hero, "You're a Ruettiger! There's nothing in the world wrong with being a Ruettiger!" He gets in after two years of junior college. He makes the team. His tenacity on the field lands one of the star running backs, played by Vince Vaughn in *Rudy* (1993), on the scout team. He gets in the last game of the season. He gets a sack on the Georgia Tech quarterback and is carried off the field. A story of confidence, commitment, character, courage, and contribution. A Hero can change their future if they want it badly enough and are willing to do whatever it takes to get there. Ru-dy! Ru-dy! Ru-dy!

We need a Hero CEO. I worked directly for a Hero—nicknamed him "Big Daddy"—for four years. While mothers will always be our number one heroes, fathers and father figures are teachers, mentors, protectors, and providers. Their commitments drive them to make sacrifices at all costs. Sigmund Freud reinforces this prevailing convention: "I cannot think of any need in childhood as strong as the need for a father's protection."[18] Big Daddy was our father and a Hero in the organization. Of course, he created the company himself while he was in postgraduate study. He would do "bed checks" on Fridays at six in the evening, give assignments (sometimes the same one to multiple leaders), and expect us to present our plans first thing Saturday morning. He built businesses, had businesses fail, engaged in battles internally and externally, built businesses back up again, and always ended up better off. He also had a bit of a "white knight" in him. An errant knight who has broken away to wander on adventures. Our corporate Sir Galahad is the most innocent, morally good, and likely to find the Holy Grail. I was hooked.

---

18 Sigmund Freud, *Civilization and Its Discontents* (W. W. Norton & Company, 2005).

Despite leaving the company (yeah, let's call it "being fired"), I am still hooked on Big Daddy.

I have also had my fair share of Heroes in my leadership teams. Three come to mind. Two found realignment; the third is my biggest regret—I wasn't able to relieve them of their duties effectively. I inherited the first leader who was extraordinarily remarkable for their strong moral compass, bravery, determination, and resilience. Let's call them Alan. Alan was confident, and rightfully so, because they were highly talented. They were a warrior hero. They fought for seven years to fix the organization before I arrived. It never quite got there, but they had successes and the scars to prove it. Through all those trials and tribulations, Alan developed credibility and a reputation inside and outside the organization for incredible strength, courage, and being able to do the impossible. They were tough inside and out. They didn't let an obstacle get in their way. They kicked butt and took names during the difficult times (times that lingered until I arrived as the brand-new, first-time CEO).

Complex journeys will even wear out the superhero. Hawkeye quits the Avengers after his near-death experience (to take care of his family instead of risking his life), and we are never quite sure why Iron Man does the same. Too much time in a financial turnaround will beat down the best senior leaders and damage any team. Alan was wary after the previous seven years. The organization—board and leadership—weren't up for them either. Alan had become overbearing, a bit too boastful, arrogant, possessive of the past and people, moody, manipulative, and more than a bit selfish. They also became restless and sought out the prior CEO to join them in their next adventure. When Alan came to my office, going or staying wasn't a choice. There was no choice. Alan needed to rid themselves of the past and find a new Hero's adventure. The organization needed a different personality and skill set to move forward effectively and healthily.

The next Hero was one I hired. Let's call them Linda. They followed a literal saint of a leader who had served the organization faithfully through lots of turmoil with calm, aplomb, and nobility. I loved that leader. Still do after their passing. They were suddenly diagnosed with a brain tumor and decided it was best to step down. So, we promoted Linda from another market. Great references. They walked on water. We did our best, including the entire team, my entire family, and the broader community, to make them feel warm and welcome. Once they settled in, we found ourselves with a Byronic hero (named after the English romantic poet Lord Byron). Linda's life was a series of travels over vast settings and several careers. They had radically altered their lifestyle and commitments in service to God. The more, the better. The farther away, the better. The more different, the better. Distance made this Hero's life and actions more illustrious. They possessed a rich life but kept it buried as an inner life under the surface. However, on the outside, they were prickly, without a sense of humor, pouting, resentful, cryptic, enigmatic, and unreadable. They alienated themselves from everything and everyone with intent. Then, it got worse. Linda started to covertly question—behind everyone's back, including mine—the conventions, beliefs, actions, and norms of me, the team, and the organization. It fell flat when Linda went for broader support to change others and the company. It was everyone else who needed to change, not them, of course. Despite their virtuous and sympathetic traits and ambitions, Linda turned from a Byronic hero to a tragic hero. What could we do to help them and fix the tragedy? We moved Linda to yet another market. As that unfolded, it was the same chapter and verse. Linda failed miserably. For all the same reasons, they failed before they landed with me. I was a willing and naïve new boss. These types of Heroes possess profound passion and morals, but they are also profoundly wounded. They continue to experience the same exact failures and fate (past, present, and future) until they own and deal with their fatal flaws.

This last practical example rivals Beowulf, Siegfried, Gilgamesh, and Rama, all put together in one epic leadership mess. I inherited them and then promoted them. What was I thinking? They were of "noble birth" like the great heroes of old. This leader, whom I will call Phil, gave off a sense of integrity, courage, and compassion. Phil put on the air of being well loved and someone who was solely interested in always doing the right thing. Well, after all, commoners make for only average Heroes. Phil fit nicely into the liberator Hero mold. Their goal was to liberate others and themselves from what they perceived as a broken system. Always striving to help everyone break away from bondage. Imagine Moses in the desert for forty years, moving from Egypt to Israel and the Promised Land. If you pull out a map, the distance is only about 430 miles. At five miles a day, it should have only taken eighty-six days (yes, less than three months). This leader, too, was directionally challenged. Phil did things differently to do things differently. With no direction, no transparency, no urgency, and no accountability. No results at all, either. Some saw them as hopeful and optimistic, believing in their convictions about freedom. Who doesn't want more autonomy? Phil never accepted defeat.

I would often tell others that Phil created the swirl of organizational attention deficit hyperactivity disorder around them. They were not expansive in their thinking, never making room for truths other than their own. Phil consistently failed to plan adequately. Odysseus had the Cyclops. Beowulf had Grendel. This Hero built up everyone above them in title and position as a supernatural foe. They were fighting leaders who weren't mere mortals. A superhuman boss enemy.

Their sense of justice completely blinded their ego and overconfidence. They elicited great forces in this battle and took pride in the fact that success would mean they would be celebrated by everyone everywhere for their victory. While trying to avoid my heroic quest for truth with this leader and their ultimate demise, I am comforted by the words of Sylvester Stallone, "There's a natural law of karma that vindictive people, who go out of their way to hurt others, will end up broke and alone."[19] Best of luck to my Cyclops.

Firing the Hero

To dump the Hero, you have to be the anti-Hero. To get into the right frame of mind for freeing up their future, put on "Anti-Hero" really loud (from Taylor Swift's tenth studio album, *Midnights*, from 2022). I particularly love this song. I bought the shirt when I saw her live. You know the song. It's the one about who the problem really is, and it fits your Hero leadership situation.

Inspired by Swift's insecurities and projecting yours as well, the lyrics focus on the impact of fame (you are famous because you are the leader) and self-loathing (you are criticizing yourself about not dealing with this person or hiring them in the first place, let alone promoting them). Go directly against the Hero's narrative, and don't look back. Now is the time to be Tony Soprano. You don't need strong morals, courage, or selflessness right now. Be selfish for you, your team, and the organization. Rebel against the Hero's journey. No more delaying.

The Hero has made their fatal mistake, and there is no going back. Hubris is every Hero's fatal flaw. Too much pride. Too much

19 "Sylvester Stallone Quotes," BrainyQuote, https://www.brainyquote.com/quotes/sylvester_stallone_584128.

confidence. Odysseus was arrogant, disrespectful, conceited, rude, and manipulative. This made him do dumb things. Same with the "white knight." In all their pride, they were always on missions and had a compulsive (even obsessive) need to rescue others from their actual or perceived failures. The knight is the only one to save the day. Everyone else (yes, the entire planet) is helpless, vulnerable, and damaged.

The Hero commits the major leadership sin. Even the most epic Heroes, at some point, commit the major team sin. They can't help themselves. They are not loyal to you. They are not loyal to the team and the organization. Their only loyalty is to themselves and their cause. I once had a salty, smoky, and fatty (more figuratively than literally) team member, a complete rebel without a cause who reported to me. This person scolded me in front of the entire team: "You expect trust [and loyalty] to be given to you because of your title and position. Trust [and loyalty] are earned and given." Take that.

That is a very shallow, immature, and artless outlook on trust and loyalty. Loyalty, for this purpose, does not have an on-and-off switch. You aren't either loyal or disloyal. You aren't either completely trustworthy or completely untrustworthy. It is a continuum. I have a great friend and former colleague whom I can trust with anything except when it comes to the matter of money. I mistook money for across-the-board trust. After finding the error in my ways and reconciling our relationship, I can talk about anything with them, except for anything that even remotely resembles dollars.

You should absolutely demand loyalty from your team. It does come with your title and position (and being their boss). Yes, a leader must inspire loyalty (and trust). It comes from walking the talk. Being strong, disciplined, courageous, having purpose, and acting with purpose and direction. Own it. All of it (even when you had nothing to do with it), including the process and the results. Model how to take responsibility and accountability. My grandmother once said, "He is not my President." I get that she didn't vote for the winner. Win or lose, you support the person, position, and title. They earned it.

Loyalty—given and earned—is critical to leadership. Loyalty and trust are about commitment and strong (and deep) relationships. Loyalty is the lifeblood of organizations. It is the glue that shapes the growth and success of all people, all organizations, all cultures, and all societies. In *The Five Dysfunctions of a Team: A Leadership Fable*, Patrick Lencioni asserts that trust is a team's bedrock. Without trust, you don't get healthy conflict, commitment, accountability, and meaningful results as a team. And its cousin, loyalty. When your Hero gets engrossed in their ego, champions their causes, and shows their disloyalty, do yourself a favor and get them out of the organization.

While it will turn painful and personal, take care of the present. Leave the last chapters of the Hero's journey to a higher power. Take comfort in the words of Father Cavanaugh (played by Ned Beatty) delivered to Rudy in one of the front pews of the Basilica of the Sacred Heart at Notre Dame: "Son, in thirty-five years of religious study, I've come up with only two hard, incontrovertible facts—there is a God, and I'm not Him."

TAKEAWAYS

- If you want to take the Hero out, you will have to become the anti-Hero.
- Keep an eye out for the Hero's hubris.
- Remember that as a leader, you automatically deserve loyalty.

WHAT'S NEXT

Next, we will look at the Caregiver—and as you've probably guessed by now, we will fire them.

CHAPTER 9

THE CAREGIVER

God gave burdens; He also gave shoulders. –Yiddish proverb

THE CAREGIVER

The Caregiver protects and cares for others, rooted in their natural compassion, nurturing, and generosity.

Eating Campbell's soup on a cold, snowy evening. Simple yet not-so-simple Mary Poppins.

The Caregiver is the most gripping archetype I have experienced. Buckle your seat belt and hang on to your seat. My two most personal examples and two most practical and intoxicating (and personally satisfying) examples of deep-sixing leaders sit right here in this domain.

Our youngest son is kind, compassionate, empathetic, trusting, and humble. He always acts with good intentions (well, more often than not), and his intentions keep him focused on his goals. One of his goals is to protect and always keep the peace. He has strong intuition and opinions on what's going on in the lives of others. He doesn't want anything bad to happen to the people he is close to (family and friends). He can tell what others need even when they don't ask. He will give everything to prevent harm from coming to others. He gets this from his mother (definitely not even one teaspoonful from me). My wife, too, is generous, optimistic, transparent, and open. She is gracious, giving, and helpful, so much so that strangers instantly connect with her. Within fifteen minutes of meeting her, the stranger opens up completely, shares their entire life story, and shows a side of themselves that very few in their intimate life even know. More often than not, tears and counseling are involved. Others purposely seek out her care, wisdom, advice, and love. It can sometimes be a burden for her and those around her (like me, who gets engrossed in the "drama").

Based on the 1980s television series of the same name, the 2014 movie *The Equalizer* features Denzel Washington as Robert McCall. McCall, a gentle and harmless older man, is a retired special forces agent who now works at a Boston hardware store. He loves helping people, especially those struggling in life and searching for a different future. He is traditional, logical, practical, loyal, reliable, and exceptionally dedicated. He shows up when he says he will and keeps his every promise. At the same time, Denzel plays a character who is questioning his principles and morality. He is in conflict with himself and living somewhere between his past and present lives. The series of movies is brutally violent, born out of McCall's compelling sense of justice.

Look no further than the late Mother Theresa. Mary Teresa Bojaxhiu was born in Albania, moved to Ireland at eighteen, and settled in India for most of her life, where she founded the Missionaries of Charity. The Missionaries provide care, without charge, for sick and abandoned children, the aged, the convalescent, refugees, the mentally ill, people with AIDS, former prostitutes, and people with leprosy. She was an unwaveringly caring, respectful, loyal, altruistic, empathetic, hardworking, motivated, and driven servant. Like all leaders, she had her share of critics long after passing at age eighty-seven in 1997 in Kolkata. Revered globally for her boundless generosity and selflessness, Mother Theresa was canonized a saint by the Roman Catholic Church, and her feast day is September 5 (the anniversary of her death).

When Caregivers Go Wrong

My first personal example is a leader in a missional and values-driven leadership role who took on the persona of a guardian Caregiver. Let's call them Doug. They were a parent-like figure in my life as the CEO, as well as many others in this organizational story. Doug focused on the customer and the team's needs as a visible role model. They ensured those they guarded remained safe and secure. They had this unique proclivity for starting initiatives internally and partnering with community organizations in a way that demanded the intensity of their time, energy, and resources (as well as the company's significant investment in their follies). In their quenchless thirst to fix all of the world's problems and keep everyone happy, Doug found it hard to say no to people and priorities. When things turned rough, it was because they overdid things. They got too close to people—in a way that was unhealthy for the leader—and skirted the lines of harassment, bullying, mistreatment, aggression, abuse, and workplace molestation. Their prior felonies are also featured prominently in the Lover chapter. Finding themselves stretched too thin and incapable of delivering on promises, they spent organizational resources in wild, reckless, and wasteful ways. While I inherited this leader and was close to them to the very end, a closer look into their past uncovered a long, unfortunate track record of a bright and capable leader who failed to help those who needed it most. Their help was always conducted in an irresponsible and self-centered way with unproductive and destructive approaches, a shadow of dubiousness, and unfortunate endings, especially for them.

The second Caregiver leader (let's call them Stephanie) helped cover up the gross transgressions of the leader profiled above. The old British proverb (a version of the phrase that appeared in 1545 in William Turner's satire *The Rescuing of Romish Fox*) rings proper here: "Birds of a feather flock together." The whole adage ends with, "… until the cat comes." Licking my paws and meowing. However, this isn't where things went ferociously wrong. Stephanie was in a highly people-forward role (especially at the immediate start of the topsy-turvy COVID-19 outbreak) and vividly relished the role of the Samaritan. They did things simply because it was the right thing to do. There was a purity and innocence about them, their thoughts, their words, and their approaches. Not needing recognition or praise, they were always looking for ways to help others. However, they were always willing to accept recognition when given. They got out of the gate in the organization with a flash, a flurry, substance, and meaning, quickly turning into one of the highest-potential, high-performance, and highly recognized leaders in the entire organization. Then, the pandemic hit, and something flipped. Just like a light switch. Like nothing I have seen before or since. They pushed themselves without understanding their limits. They put themselves in harm's way on purpose. They paralyzed themselves. Stephanie stopped listening, stopped doing anything at all, and purposely damaged relationships with their peers and boss in the process.

The Caregiver can get to a place where they long to be a martyr. It happened right in front of me. Because the best way to show their caring and compassionate nature was to—literally and metaphorically—become a martyr for the team and the organization. They guilt-tripped others when the martyrdom wasn't appreciated or embraced. As they turned more resentful and went backward in their results, the team responded to this behavior by placing too many demands on the innocent guardian.

There was an event where I publicly called out (with good intent and most of it a healthy admonishment, while at times I overstepped my bounds) these behaviors and the exact issues impinging on this leader's ability to continue on the team. Talk about the cleanup I needed to do. I gave the martyr exactly what they were looking for. After their tumultuous departure, people came out of the woodwork to share this leader's use of poisonous cliques and revenge with their peers and those below them. The team called her "The Mean Girl," as in *Mean Girls*, the 2004 teen comedy starring Lindsay Lohan. The best way I can describe this individual is in the words of Hugh Grant: "I get very annoyed when people think I'm nice or diffident or a polite

English gentleman. I'm a nasty piece of work, and people should know that."[20] A nasty piece of work!

Both of these Caregiver leaders were highly adept at using referent and coercive power to their advantage—both overtly and covertly, with good intention and with malice. They were proficient at building solid relationships with the boss and other high positions of formal and informal power within the organization. They would influence their own followers by name-dropping, quoting, and directly referencing the boss to seize on the boss's admiration, respect, and identification (i.e., referent power). When that didn't work, or they needed to apply more elbow grease, they would exert force, threats, and other forms of coercion, laying the coercion right at the feet of the boss, to stimulate their desired outcome. You don't want leaders on your team who use your name passively (worse yet, aggressively) or in vain to get something they want. I make enough mistakes on my own and don't need to borrow others' mistakes. It would be best if you never used your boss's name or the board's name to get what you want. This is an immature distraction and an unmistakable lack of accountability. Don't pin your lack of performance, poor decision-making, and lack of leadership on someone or something else.

Careers for the Caregiver

The Caregiver can be the backbone of an organization. A seemingly selfish and uncaring business world desires love, kindness, comfort,

20 Caroline Graham, "Hugh Grant Admits He's Nothing Like His Endearing On-Screen Roles," *Daily Mail*, August 27, 2016, https://www.dailymail.co.uk/news/article-3761656/I-annoyed-people-think-m-polite-Englishman-m-nasty-piece-work-freeze-hear-word-Action-Hugh-Grant-admits-s-like-endearing-screen-roles.html.

support, and protection. This type of leader's care, compassion, and nurturing are most often found in healthcare and organizations that serve children, older adults, the poor, and the vulnerable. You will see these individuals line up for important roles in HR, philanthropy, community and economic development, and mission and values. Suitable matches for this archetype are areas that require service, advice, listening, reassurance, and an open heart. In their sweet spot, Caregivers give you the best of self-sacrifice, patience, high levels of competence, generosity, and the ability to successfully multitask with efficiency and results.

Victims and Martyrs

What you don't need, as a leader, is a martyr. You don't need victims. Martyrs and victims judge others rather than deal with their flaws and weaknesses. They find others who are equally pessimistic and supercharge this clique against everyone else. Victims and martyrs believe they are the only ones doing their jobs. At the same time, they spend most of their time complaining rather than committing themselves to and diligently doing the challenging work. They tried that before. It just can't be done. Only the government, an organizational partner, or the board could solve their woes. They are helpless, so they create narratives that justify them not doing anything. While the narratives are likely true, they aren't the real story. It is all a distraction from them.

I have landed in organizations where the team is full of victims and martyrs. You will find these teams throwing themselves to the lions in challenging industries, competitive markets, or where organizational viability is at peril. These organizations can't spell "abundance." Setbacks and obstacles are a product of things entirely outside their control. They limit the organization by the leadership's beliefs and behaviors (in shaping their reality, which is rarely *the* reality). What they seek is sympathy and control, as well as to manipulate and avoid responsibility. Ultimately, they land in a place where no possibility is possible. It becomes a self-fulfilling prophecy unless someone puts a stop to the cycle.

Suppose you are in a martyr organization, or you are dealing with a victim leader. In that case, you have to steer them back to reality, not their past life or perceived one. Back to the opportunities (not staying stuck or in stagnation). This takes time. A lot of your time. You will have to elicit help from a non-victim team member or, preferably, seek outside help to keep harping on the message. Take away the outside forces creating problems. Insist that something has to be done. It would be best if you controlled the discussion and the messaging. The team will hate it. The individual will hate it and hate you. You deserve medals if you can get them to understand what is happening. Your cause is saving the team and the organization from the death spiral. If you can't fix it, exit the individual or start martyring the victims in a sweeping motion.

TAKEAWAYS

- Distinguish between healthy Caregivers and toxic martyrs.
- Recognize when Caregivers start attributing all their failures to external forces.
- As a leader, choose to intervene from the start.

WHAT'S NEXT

Next, we'll look at the Explorer: thrills, chills, and possible trouble.

CHAPTER 10

THE EXPLORER

If your ego starts out, "I am important, I am big, I am special," you're in for some disappointments when you look around at what we've discovered about the universe. No, you're not big. No, you're not. You're small in time and in space. And you have this frail vessel called the human body that's limited on Earth. –**Neil deGrasse Tyson**

THE EXPLORER

The Explorer loves thrills, risks, discoveries, and traveling the world.

Think of the Red Bull brand.

Indiana Jones.

Hernán Cortés de Monroy y Pizarro Altamirano, born into a family of lesser nobility in Spain, sought a life of adventure and riches in the New World. His dreams came true as he became a central figure in the economic, political, and military environment in the Americas in the sixteenth century. His exploration toppled the Aztec Empire and brought what is now Mexico under the control of the King of Castile. A popular legend says he burned his ships in Veracruz after landing. I've used this example in a team advance as an analogy to signal that we will achieve our intention or die trying.

That's the positive, history book spin on Cortés. The explorer was well known for his intelligence, cleverness, and honor. He loved taking significant risks and pushing boundaries. He was also described as haughty and ruthless. To many Mexicans, Cortés is the poster child for rape and plunder. He tore down Tenochtitlan. He hanged the Aztec warrior Cuauhtémoc. He imposed Spanish rule over the Indigenous peoples. It is said today that the country and its people have still not been able to move past this historic conquest. Add to that, he was suspected of murdering Spanish government officials to get his way. It is also speculated that he ordered his ships destroyed to avoid paying the loans on them. Another theory is that they did not burn their ships at all but dismantled them for the essential parts of the vessels. By all accounts, Cortés was a formidable leader while, at the same time, defiant, arrogant, self-serving, greedy, and generally indifferent.

On a high-flying note, Bessie Coleman was the first African American and Native American woman to earn her pilot's license. Born in 1892 in Texas, she attended college in Oklahoma and beauty school in Chicago. She heard stories from her brothers and soldiers who had fought in World War I about France, flying, and opportunities for women overseas. After her applications were rejected at flight schools in the United States, she learned French in night school, wrote applications in that language, and landed acceptance at the Caudron Brothers' School of Aviation in Le Crotoy, where she earned her international pilot's license in 1921. She returned to the United States to buy her own plane, open her own flight school, and gain a reputation for her pilot prowess and acrobatic flying. At the age of 36, Coleman fell two thousand feet to her death while preparing her aerial stunts for a flight show in Jacksonville.

Explorers find themselves by discovering the world around them. They make the most of their experiences and adapt to changing circumstances without a second thought. They are focused, prepared, persevering, creative, highly inquisitive, curious, composed, and resilient, and they live every moment, interaction, and initiative with a strong sense of conviction. Explorers are on your team to break boundaries and grow the organization. All these strengths can turn into flaws (even fatal in some circumstances, like in the case of Cortés and Bessie) when executed in excess. In their pursuit of things on their own and in their own direction, they risk mutiny within their teams. They are not team players. They aren't exceptionally skilled at communicating their knowledge and teaching the rest of their teams. At times, they will stand out and become obvious misfits. Please don't make the mistake of fencing them in when things go wrong. That is when they will go rogue, with a gross lack of preparation, planning, and focus. When not managed, you will find yourself wandering aimlessly with the Explorer, with the team ready to rise up against both of you.

Over the past two decades, I have hired young leaders straight from graduate school to learn and contribute to the organization. It was always an opportunity to inject and invest in diverse leadership in the organization for the long haul (well after I retired). The hope was that they would perform and connect with more senior leaders in the organization to find opportunities after that year of fellowship. One of my COOs loved hiring them for another year and giving them intense exposure to real-world operations. Many still work in the organizations in which we hired them. A few have already risen to CEO roles. There is only one in that history whom I have had to let go.

They Came, They Saw, and They Tried to Conquer

That "only one" was an Explorer. I (we all) missed that in the interview process. The Explorer can be great when leading strategy, business development, or marketing. They are the direct opposite of remarkable when joining an organization for a test period with no actual work experience before joining the organization. This individual yearned to escape the mundane and break free from the typical confines of this new leadership role. Unfortunately, the role is meant to be prosaic. It is intended to test if you can manage whatever is thrown your way. The role involved managing senior team meetings, including preparing agendas, pre-reading materials, post-meeting minutes, and communications, as well as managing the mechanics of the board agenda and packet with the CEO and their executive assistant. The role included taking on projects that no one else wanted to—such as budget support for the CFO, analyzing departmental process issues, or project management for the organizational strategic plan.

You shouldn't skip steps when you are a leader. Pay your dues. I fought that one at the same age as this individual. However, I played the game, and it paid off. This individual ignored directions. Missed deadlines. Just didn't do things. Delegated their work to others. The one downside of delegation is that no one reported to them. They were downright rude—born out of a strong sense of entitlement to anyone and everyone, including me at the end. We cut our losses in that first test year. Yeah, they were done, done, and done. Some other company can benefit from their independence, freedom, sense of adventure, disregard for boundaries, and discovery of new (and non-value-added) things.

There is also a senior leader in an operational leadership role leading significant revenue and the bottom line. Uh-oh. For the expedition, they recruited a team that was exactly like them. Their quest to find themselves, help others find themselves, create a fulfilling life, work in the frontier between the known and unknown, and conquer new territories was incredibly alluring. This transformational voyage was attractive to governance, leaders, the community, and potential donors. The leadership attracted quite a deep-seated followership. I have to give them credit for bringing fascinating and genuinely novel concepts to the table. Who isn't excited about the leader who livestreams themselves to lead workouts for employees? Or plans to spend $500 million in capital that doesn't grow revenue or reduce expenses? Or creates partnerships to build out a service that would never produce a positive (or even breakeven) profit? Oh, wait, I almost forgot that all these wild explorations always hit the media before the initiatives went through higher leadership and governance approval (or, in most cases, had even been discussed outside of their team).

The more you peeled back the onion on this Explorer, the more unpleasant smells took over the room. Much like Shrek. In all the hype, everyone (other than them) got left in the lurch. Operations were poor. Engagement was poor. The quality and service of the products were mixed. I think the results could have been different if the individual had shown up in the office more than one day a week. Then again, maybe not. Explorers, in their shadows, lack commitment (to the organization and the team), have no real direction (other than their own), pursue autonomy (rather than balancing it with collaboration) at the expense of others, and become increasingly self-indulgent. The critical and needed stakeholders were disenfranchised and had stopped bringing issues forward. Why? Because others saw their following and refused to swim against the tide. Unfortunately, the blind followers didn't know the financial situation. They didn't realize competitors were growing revenue faster and stealing market share monthly. They didn't realize engagement was the lowest in the company, and people didn't want to work with the Explorer and their team. It was a five-year free fall. To be fair, there were great press releases, social media videos, and plans destined to drain the broader company's resources for years to come.

Let's call this Explorer Captain Robert Falcon Scott. Scott was a British Royal Navy officer whose name became synonymous with Antarctica. We owe so many scientific and geographical discoveries to his twelve-year commitment to the exploration of the seventh continent. The captain embarked on his final adventure in 1910, which got off to a miserable start with the sinking of the team's ship. There were signs, yet Scott pressed on. The last entry in his journal was on March 29, 1912, when he was the last of three in his team to die. Temperatures became unseasonably cold. A blizzard had arrived. Communication and planning throughout the entire expedition were confusing at best. They ran out of food and fuel, even though they were only eleven miles from a massive supply of both. Their original stores were light on vitamins C and D, making them susceptible to scurvy. Scott ignored the tried-and-true dog sleds on this tour. Instead, they tried a new technology: motor sleds that were early in their development and had never been tried in Antarctica. He also preferred using Siberian ponies that hadn't been tested at the South Pole. He never bothered to train his team to use the ponies. Antarctica isn't Siberia. Captain Scott was the right person with the wrong plan, in the wrong place, and at the wrong time. The entire team lost their lives.

Our leadership decisions aren't quite life or death. Thankfully so. But the Explorer's spectrum can run from good to evil. A quest to understand the world can change a team, organization, community, and maybe even the world around us for good. Another pursuit could lead to the undoing of everything around them. For my past Explorer, one of their fancies is still operating at significant financial losses a decade later, with no signs of hope for black rather than red. The organization has never really recovered from ten years of operational neglect. Fortunately, we nixed the $500+ million homage to their leadership.

How to Fire the Explorer

The Explorer is an especially difficult archetype to manage out of an organization. They are highly resilient souls. Others rally around their determination and ability to overcome obstacles to conquer vast plans. When put in the corner, they fight with Attila and the Hun-like hordes, using organizational battering rams, siege towers, and mining to breach your walls. It is personal and not even remotely about the real issues. The big, sinister corporation and its leaders are taking it out on the one leader who dares to challenge authority and wants to do things differently. That puts you squarely up against everything that is pure, good, American—authentic freedom, innovation, self-discovery, beating all the odds, baseball, hot dogs, apple pie, and Chevrolet. Be prepared for some wild, rocky, and trailblazing paths on this pink-slip journey as you go against everything that is American.

Don't try to talk your way out of the adventurous spirit of the Explorer. Their message is captivating, and your message is a no-win strategy. Instead, spend your time appealing to all the diverse stakeholders, especially those stuck managing the details for (and without any support from) the Explorer. Keep your message consistent, both qualitative and quantitative. Show the numbers. Bring the people with the anecdotes about what isn't working to the table. Balance their allure of exploration with stability and trustworthiness. As you continue to press harmoniously, the Explorer will be more contradictory and self-contradictory. The practicality of your decision and a future without Captain Scott will be muddy in the heat of the moment. Time (i.e., water under the bridge), perseverance, and veracity are the best gifts for making this change.

Our Explorer landed with another familiar organization. I warned the organization. Many people involved warned them. The track record warned them. Past employers on this Explorer's resume had the very same issues with this leader, which had led to their departure. Explorers interview exceptionally well with their grand portrayal of a sexy future that only they can deliver. And they do get off to a blazing start when hired. I wish we hadn't wasted a decade (for me, two long years) and the new organization had heeded our animated and emphatic warnings. Wild visions never became a reality. The captivated network of supporters from their past didn't follow them to the new organization. Operational challenges surfaced where they had never existed before. They paralyzed another organization. Done again and again.

Our two-time failed Explorer offers an immutable lesson for hiring and dehiring. The world of CEOs is like the world of football coaches. In acts of utter desperation, organizations and football teams go back and forth with mid-tier leaders dooming themselves, their success, and their future—time after time. After four years as head football coach at the University of Louisville, Bobby Petrino left the Bluegrass State for the NFL and the Atlanta Falcons. Not even a full first season, and he accepted the head coaching job for the Arkansas Razorbacks. With a 5–7 start in 2008, he took the program on a meteoric rise with three straight bowl appearances (including the prestigious Sugar Bowl—I was at that game—and the Cotton Bowl) and two straight ten-win seasons. In the offseason after the Cotton Bowl victory in 2012, Petrino was involved in a motorcycle accident that turned into an escapade. He was riding with a former All-Southeastern Conference volleyball player whom he had hired a week earlier as a student-athlete development coordinator for the football program. Explorer archetype gone bad? Oops, like really bad. If you had put the decision about what to do with the head coach to a referendum in Arkansas, he would still be the head coach. A year later, Western Kentucky hired him as its head coach. He coached for a year, and Louisville hired him back as its head coach for four seasons. You read that right. The Cardinals didn't like the results (surprise, surprise), and they realigned their football staff. He then landed at Missouri State as head coach for three seasons. Next was an assistant position at the University of Nevada, Las Vegas. For twenty days. Texas A&M came calling, and he led the offense for one season. Get this: After major changes in the coaching ranks at A&M, he accepted the role of offensive coordinator at … wait, for it … the University of Arkansas. Woo Pig Sooie!

I am all for reconciliation, redemption, and forgiveness. God knows, I need it. More than most. But, as Albert Einstein is often attributed as saying (but never said), "Insanity is doing the same thing over and over again and expecting different results." What we know Einstein did say was, "God does not play dice with the universe."[21] You shouldn't play dice with Explorers.

21 Mindy Weisberger, "'God Plays Dice with the Universe,' Einstein Writes in Letter About His Qualms with Quantum Theory," Live Science, June 12, 2019, https://www.livescience.com/65697-einstein-letters-quantum-physics.html.

TAKEAWAYS

- Anticipate having to fight an Explorer about their termination.
- Focus on the data that will give you evidence of the Explorer's failures.
- Look out for patterns in the Explorer's track record.

WHAT'S NEXT

Next, we'll look at the Ruler, and more specifically, the Ruler gone bad.

CHAPTER 11

THE RULER

I suppose leadership at one time meant muscles, but today it means getting along with people. –Mahatma Gandhi

THE RULER

Creating from the chaos, the Ruler is typically controlling, stern, responsible, and organized.
Think of how and why a Mercedes-Benz looks, feels, and drives better than the rest.
Mr. Burns from *The Simpsons.*

This is the most fun of all the twelve people you can and will encounter in your leadership journey. The Italian poet Dante Alighieri completed the *Divine Comedy* way back in 1321. This work has inspired many others in their exploration of heaven, hell, and purgatory over the past eight centuries. Instead of Latin being accessible to only the most educated, Dante delivered one of the most incredible works in Western literature in the Italian language.

Dante's nine circles of Hell, featured in the *Inferno* section of the masterpiece, ring something like the seven deadly sins, Jung's archetypes (not published until six hundred years later, in 1919), and the people who get in the way of your and your organization's success. That is not a coincidence. The first eight circles, in order, are limbo, lust, gluttony, greed, wrath, heresy, violence, and fraud.[22]

Let's zero in on Dante's ninth circle of Hell for the Ruler gone bad. It's not excruciatingly hot here. If you land in this place in the afterlife, picture being unable to move, with your lower half frozen in a lake. You have the pleasure of spending all eternity with the angel that betrayed God (the Devil, also known as Satan or Lucifer), featured in the center of the lake. That's a bonus. This circle is divided into four rounds in which you are placed according to the seriousness of your transgressions. Your body is deeper in the ice based on your assigned round.

Round one is named Caina after Cain, who killed his brother Abel (The Bible's Book of Genesis). Round two is named Antenora after Anthenor of Troy, who was Priam's counselor during the Trojan War and famously betrayed the Greeks (Homer's *Iliad*). Round three is named Ptolomaea after Ptolemy, son of Abubus, who invited Simon, the priest, and his two sons to dinner and then, of all things,

---

22 Dante Alighieri, *The Divine Comedy: Inferno, Purgatory, and Paradise*, c. 1321.

killed them (the Torah's Book of Maccabees). Round four is named Judecca after Judas Iscariot, the apostle who betrayed Jesus with a kiss in the garden (U2's "Until the End of the World" is the conversation between Jesus and Judas).

Yes, the ninth circle of Hell is reserved for treachery. From Dante's perspective, the worst sinners were those who betrayed their loved ones, their countries (expand this to their organizations and their bosses), and their God. Killed their brother, killed their army, killed an entire family, and killed the Son of God. But these aren't simply crimes. Treachery is a sin of the heart. A profound violation of trust with a penetrating sense of faithlessness. Trickery. Cheating. Deceit. Sabotage. The old double-cross. Breaking confidence. Sweet talk. Dirty dealing. Grift. Rackets. Scams. Selling out. Outright treason.

Despite the sentence to the innermost ring of Hell (the lowest, darkest, and farthest from Heaven), the charge of betrayal has become all too common. Theodore Hall was a well-heeled and brilliant physicist with degrees from Harvard and the University of Chicago. His father was a furrier, and he had emigrated to America to escape anti-Semitism in Russia. His mother was a second-generation Russian Jew who died when he was a teenager. Hall was part of the team responsible for the race to develop the first and second atomic bombs during World War II. While J. Robert Oppenheimer and others were being accused of spying, Theodore was the one providing detailed descriptions and tactics related to the "Fat Man" bomb (the one dropped on Nagasaki) to the Soviets.

Mufasa is the bona fide ruler in Disney's *The Lion King*. The lion king understands the world around him and the gravity of the circle of life (regardless of a creature's status in his kingdom). His character even looks strong, brave, wise, and balanced. His majestic and royal exterior is boosted by being kindhearted, playful, an understanding father, and a loving family member. He is highly respected and revered by the vast majority of animals. He trusts his brother, Scar, who doesn't feel the same way. That is perhaps Mufasa's only flaw. Scar wants the throne. So, his schemes with the hyenas finally kill Mufasa. Scar's fatal leadership flaw is his ego. He is eager to be the most intelligent and accomplished. The absolute best tyrant without apology. Scar, not surprisingly, fails the kingdom, and the hungry hyenas ensure his ultimate demise.

Rulers Gone Wrong

Fortunately, and unfortunately, I have never had to let someone go for betraying me, for trying to knock me off in a wildebeest stampede, the organization, or God, or whatever higher being you believe in. However, there are two individuals whom I have had the pleasure of working with as peers who fit the Mufasa mold.

One of the accused appeared very professional, well put together, overtly friendly, flattering, and complimentary. Engaging and inclusive. They loved the spotlight and being the life of the party. Promptly taking credit for all that was good and, at the same time, pinning the blame on others when things went even mildly wrong. In small circles, however, they loved talking about other people (behind their backs). As they got traction with the small gossip, they would move to putting the same people down with deeply demeaning (often personal) remarks. They were stirring up drama by spreading partial truths, gossip, and downright lies that damaged reputations. They went so far as to undermine others they perceived as more intelligent or capable. Smarts, talent, and outcomes threatened them. Whom aren't they talking about? Are they talking about us? And me, too? You bet. This "gem" went so far (on at least two occasions that are known) to threaten to quit if a specific person was hired for a job (jobs they did not apply for and were never considered for).

The other individual was a people pleaser with a dangerous streak. They were charming, polished, articulate, visionary, and seemingly deeply connected (internally and externally). They valued people and fashioned themselves as a great advocate for others, the team, the organization, and humankind. They seemed in tune with others' feelings, needs, and the prevailing flow within the organization (from the front lines to the boardroom). This was all a show and a one-way street. As my best friend says in these situations, "They would stand on your head to save themselves if both of you were drowning." He would add, "They would circle the wagons and shoot in to get ahead." This Ruler's mission was self. The image of friendliness was distorted and make-believe. They elicited accomplices to further their bad behavior. But the Ruler put them out front while they went to the back and blended with the scenery. Yes, they manipulated people to get what they wanted. They turned revengeful, spiteful, and downright rude when things didn't turn out as they wanted or to their benefit. I was in the room when they advocated overthrowing the big CEO to put the big COO in the job. The COO lost their job, and the treacherous kept rising in the organization.

Treachery, in any way, shape, or form, is serious. Betrayal is insidious. Covert and in the shadows. The harm gradually and destructively perpetuates itself to the point of no return. It kills all relationships in its view. It is organization- and life-altering. The scene is overcome with shock, loss, grief, morbid preoccupation, damaged self-esteem, self-doubt, and fury. Add to that the fact that the betrayer (let's call them Judas) sincerely believes all their actions are OK. They aren't going to offer justification. Instead, they will demand expectations and apologies from you, the injured and aggrieved. You are the problem. Not them.

How to Fire the Ruler

Tolerating treachery sends the message to the organization that this behavior is acceptable and maybe even rewarded. It leads to excessive gossiping around the office, meetings after the meeting, unhealthy competition between people inside the organization, excessively late or absent employees, missed deadlines, and ignored assignments. Eventually, the good people (yes, the performers delivering results) leave and tell others inside and outside the organization exactly why they left.

So, deal with it. Right away. Don't get distracted by Judas's kiss, and stay focused. Get all the facts absolutely straight. Confront the treason head-on, but don't expect to get any movement forward. Cain killed Abel over jealousy that God liked Abel's sacrifice more. Cain expressed no remorse for his actions. That is how it works with this archetype. God punished Cain by condemning him to a life of wandering. Clearly cut them off from others and the organization. No need to respond to their blame and gossip (even when it is damaging to your reputation). It will get heated (the opposite of the frozen lake). Avoid gossip yourself. Get out there and talk to more people than feels natural. Watch your back. Like a surgical specialist operating on a cancer patient, cut it out with a scalpel. Do it as fast as humanly and organizationally possible. Cancer spreads.

I have encountered only one case of Ruler self-treason. As Britney Spears said, "I think I sabotage myself when I don't follow through with things that are important to me. It's always been a problem of mine. I have a hard time committing to things, even if they're good for me." Dante sentences these offenders to "only" the seventh circle of Hell (also called the Hell of the Violent and Bestial), where they are transformed into thorny and[23] distorted trees. Their end doesn't end there. Their tortured souls are fed upon by harpies, foul creatures with the bodies of birds, fearsome talons, and heads of women. The trees are only permitted to speak when utterly broken and bleeding.

My leader had an impeccable resume with influential references who couldn't say enough magnificent things. I landed a rock star. Once on the ground, they had a quirky ability to know what others needed before they even realized they needed it. They listened, worked excessively hard, followed up quickly, and delivered first-class results. Then, some things shifted in their personal and professional lives, and they accordingly shifted themselves in the opposite direction. What it felt like was that they were peculiarly not doing their job to impact others and their success (me included). What it looked and sounded like was that they missed deadlines. Initiatives launched and then came to a stop without a word or an excuse. Everything in (or near) their sphere of responsibility came to a screeching halt. Like treason, it wasn't about them. There were communication issues. They didn't understand expectations. The email never arrived. Unlike treason, which hides in the shadows, this self-treason was painfully evident, as the individual and everything around them stood still, both literally and figuratively. There was a laundry list of blunders (for our HR and legal friends out there) on public display that made it smoother to free up their future. Same technique for the seventh circle as the ninth circle.

---

23 Sharon Le Fort, "Stopping Self-Sabotage: How to Get Out of Your Own Way," *Sharon Le Fort*, April 9, 2023, https://sharonlefort.com.au/musings/f/stopping-self-sabotage.

Sabotage and self-sabotage should not be commonplace in your leadership life. Remember that not everyone is sabotaging you or even sabotaging themselves. If you find yourself thinking that way, that is more about you. Seek professional help here. Don't confuse office politics with treachery. All companies have internal politics. Don't hate the players. Hate the game. However, some organizations are drowning in treason. These are the organizations that choose not to deal with it. If you find yourself working in the ninth circle, get out tomorrow.

If you have had to take action because of treachery or self-treachery, you have the mandate to laboriously invest in healing—for the team and yourself. It would be best to start by acknowledging the betrayal and the sordid mess. Share the unvarnished information. Forgive the person who committed the crime. Alexander Pope, the eighteenth-century enlightened poet and satirist, said, "To err is human; to forgive, divine." Now is not the time for revenge. Dante has that covered. Take responsibility for what happened. Allow others to surface all their feelings and emotions. Respond calmly so the situation can be resolved and left behind. Use this perfidious shared experience to enter into relationships with the team in new and refreshing ways. The chaos can generate new perspectives, encouragement, and support. After adequate time to process, change the conversation. What happened is in the past now.

TAKEAWAYS

- Letting a Ruler archetype's treacherous behavior prevail sends a message that this sort of behavior can continue unchecked.
- Keep an eye out for the Ruler's self-sabotage.
- Create a safe space for the team to process the aftermath of exiting the Ruler.

WHAT'S NEXT

Next, we'll look at the Jester, who is far from fun and games.

CHAPTER 12

THE JESTER

There is a thin line that separates laughter and pain, comedy and tragedy, humor and hurt. –**Erma Bombeck**

THE JESTER

The Jester brings joy to the world through humor, fun, and irreverence, and often likes to make some mischief.
Think M&Ms.
Steve Stifler from *American Pie* (including 2, *Wedding,* and *Reunion*).

That thin line Bombeck talks about is the exact character of the court jester, dating back to the fourteenth century. Also called the fool, the court jester was an active member of the court of a king. Jesters were masters of song, satire, stories, and physical comedy. Maybe even juggling and acrobatics. You could find them wearing brightly colored clothes and eccentric hats as part of the entertainment value. They also contributed to the household in more practical ways. Jesters were asked to do shopping, boost the army's esprit de corps during wartime, take care of the animals, keep inventories in the kitchen, and deliver mail. Remember that. It wasn't all just fun and games.

The Fool in Shakespeare's *King Lear* plays the typical role of entertaining King Lear with wit and humor. Like in most literature, this jester also symbolizes honesty and common sense. The Fool is the King's loyal and honest advisor. He has to tell the king when the king makes mistakes. Something no one else in the court can (or is willing to) do. They effectively deliver truth to power through humor, sarcasm, and irony.

Roland, the real-life court jester to King Henry II in the late 1100s, only had one skill. Farting. Each year at Christmas, Roland was obligated to perform *Unum saltum et siffletum et unum bumbulum* (one jump, whistle, and one fart) for the king's court. For this singular skill, he was given the thirty-acre Hemingstone Manor and one hundred ten acres in Suffolk. The typical English farmer only held between five and thirty acres. A medieval flatulist. What's your unique talent?

The Joker (played most notably by Cesar Romero, Jack Nicholson, Heath Ledger and Joaquin Phoenix), in the ongoing and evolving Batman saga, is always part of the superhero's most defining moments. The violent beating and murder of Jason Todd (a ward of Batman) and the paralysis of Barbara Gordon (the daughter of Gotham City's police commissioner), to name just two. Batman represents justice and order. The Joker is an agent of chaos and fate. The Joker, in *The Dark Knight* (2008), says, "The only sensible way to live in this world is without rules."

A slightly more practical Jester is Skylar (played by Minnie Driver) in 1997's *Good Will Hunting*. This Jester is a charming and strong-willed Harvard premed student. She is wickedly (Boston) brilliant yet prefers to follow her intuition (especially regarding love). Grounded and realistic yet impulsive. While very serious about her studies and future, she is exceedingly sweet, with an infectious laugh. She has no problem dealing with Will's many eccentricities and hang-ups. She does it in a goofy, direct, and loving manner. We first meet Skylar at a bar where she meets Will for the first time. At the end of an interesting evening that almost turns into a fight in the alley, defending Skylar from a graduate student, Will walks by her on the way out, and she firmly sets the tone going forward, "You're an idiot. I've been sitting over there for forty-five minutes waiting for you to come and talk to me, but I'm tired now and I have to go home, and I couldn't sit there any more waiting for you."

Role of the Jester

Every company needs a court jester. At most, one. We need more fun at work. We land on a career that fits our obvious capabilities and what we think we are best at doing. We are rewarded for those skills, so we sharpen and hone them further. That puts us squarely in the upward pull for bigger, better, and more. At some point for all of us, our work becomes increasingly maddening and miserable. We should always be serious about work, but the stress should never exceed the joy of working collaboratively with others to make a meaningful impact.

This is the role of the Jester in our lives. The best Jesters, including Batman's Joker, if you pay close attention, are diplomats, intelligent, connected, well-informed, and keen on all the politics in the court, including the big boss. Untamed wisdom with wickedness. What a masterful combo! The Jester has very little to no actual power, but they are able to introduce "tolerated" truths (i.e., calling out the elephant in the room and that the emperor has no clothes). And with the prerogative to offer solutions and never have to execute them. Call it out, offer the path forward, and sit back and watch. Who doesn't want that job? Do you think Jim Carrey might be available (and affordable) for your team?

CEOs are not just stiffs stuffed into custom suits and shirts, Hermès ties, and Gucci shoes. They (not all) can be funny. And even a bit idiosyncratic. I am still determining if the Joker archetype works for the CEO role, but we will give it a whirl. Jason Kingsley (no, not Jason Priestley from *Beverly Hills, 90210*) is the CEO and cofounder (with his brother) of one of Europe's largest independent video game companies, Rebellion Developments, founded in 1992. If you are a gamer, you will recognize *Sniper Elite*, *Aliens vs. Predator*, and *Rainbow Six*. Otherwise, ask your kids. When not playing CEO, Kingsley loves to get on a horse, put on armor, and charge at opponents with a lance. I get the code of honor for running a company, gaming, and playing a medieval European knight on weekends. Kindness, honesty, and bravery in leadership. Who do you think plays the Jester on this senior leadership team?

The Bad Jester

I value having a Jester on my senior leadership team. I even have a tinge in me. All of them have gone extremely well except one. It was phenomenal until it wasn't. This leader was the Jester archetype like no person I had seen before or since. The best! Funny and spontaneous with a fervent zest for life. Effortlessly, the life of the party. All the time. They challenged me, the team, and our corporate norms with wit and satire. They embraced the unexpected. They made everyone around them think and laugh. How they cared about all those around them created memorable experiences with laughter, surprise, and occasional irreverence. Like no other leader (it was and still is unexplainable), they were well-informed and connected within the organization. They took the time to know every leader and what made them tick. A positive and enabling advocate for struggling leaders with the rest of the team. Always on the phone and texting to stay connected and enhance relationships. They knew what was going on in every little circle across the organization.

However, the shadow would surface on occasion, unfortunately, with the board and more senior leaders. There's that fine line again. Their humor would fall flat. Laughter with pain. They would offend critical audiences. Humor with hurt. Although they didn't report to me, I personally cautioned them for six months (at least weekly) to avoid putting me in the position of choosing between them and my bosses (the board). I constantly warned the COO (who they reported directly to) of where this would be headed without a change. I loved them. The team sorely needed them and their Jester-ness. I didn't want this to end poorly. To avoid the path they were on, they needed to focus on the core of the business and our collective priorities, not their agenda and their need to entertain. Their incessant need for humor without professionalism caused them to lose their relevance quickly. No longer fun or funny. Comedy turned to tragedy with the board calling for their head. I handed the person's head to the board on a silver platter. Well, I made the COO do the actual dirty work. Neither the COO nor the Jester owned the ending.

The Jester is not one-dimensional. They are not just there to entertain or say the things that no one else can or is willing to say. Their wit, wisdom, and cunning out-of-the-box thinking push the organization, its people, and you to new limits. It allows you to take it all to the next level. To not be stuck. They see the good in everything and everyone. That's a good thing. It is all good until those redeeming and accretive qualities manipulate and damage others. Just as fast as they can shift the momentum for the positive, they can press the brakes and bring everything to a grinding halt. Then, put things in reverse and hit the gas recklessly. Leaving a wake of destruction. Not taking anything seriously when business is serious. Catastrophic control issues. Seizing power where they had extreme power without responsibility. Cutting bad deals.

While we have popularized the Jester in our stories and literature, their fate in history is precisely what I am talking about here. The Jester's enemies (and enemies of the Jester's boss) saw this role as unessential to the overall team. High-paying and high-standing without responsibility. So, they were often an easy target. The term "don't shoot the messenger" became literal for the royal leader in constant conflict with the Jester. When the Jester crossed the line one too many times, their head would be launched by a catapult. Being a corporate Jester is similarly a dangerous job. Tread lightly with the necessary fun and funny person at work.

From day one after their departure to this day, it feels like I am living in *The Muppet Show* with Statler and Waldorf. I don't know the difference between them because they are one persona. They sit up on the balcony and heckle all the Muppets (some more than others), while Kermit, Fozzie, Beaker, and others try to put on the best show they possibly can. The dudes are snarky, take nothing and no one seriously, and foster disappointment for their own pleasure. My Statler–Waldorf is still the very best Jester. Still talks to people in the organization. Tries to manage their former areas of responsibility. Undermines and nurtures discontent. Spreads rumors and untruths. I have become Batman to their Joker. The Joker says in *Batman: The Animated Series*, "Without Batman, crime has no punchline." They need me for their ongoing punchlines.

TAKEAWAYS

- Make sure that the line between acceptable and unacceptable humor is crystal clear.
- Intervene early to make sure that Jesters do not spiral into destructive forces.
- Prepare for long-term interference from Jesters, even after termination.

WHAT'S NEXT

Next, we'll look at the Magician. Not all magic is good magic.

CHAPTER 13

THE MAGICIAN

A dream doesn't become reality through magic; it takes sweat, determination, and hard work. –**Colin Powell**

THE MAGICIAN

The Magician is seen as visionary and spiritual, wishing to make dreams a reality and create something special.
Think Disney.
Darth Vader—for the shadow aspect.

Who didn't own—or know someone who owned—a magic kit from Toys"R"Us growing up? Magicians are artists who demonstrate creativity, originality, and self-expression. We also find them to be enterprising and naturally born leaders who have that uncanny way of influencing and persuading. Harry Houdini, Dorothy Dietrich, Siegfried & Roy, Criss Angel MINDFREAK, and Penn & Teller. Delighting in the impossible.

There is a psychology around our deep fascination—one that transcends age and time—with the Magician and magic. Fantasy is always better than reality. Especially if you are a leader having to remove someone from their role. The mystery is always better than the known and certain. Magic reinvigorates that childhood wonder in all of us.

Magic is everywhere. We live in it every day. Our world is constantly being born again. We are hardwired as humans to think magically. Not to do magic. But magical thinking. Yes, our ideas, thoughts, actions, words, and symbols can influence the course of events. When logic doesn't always prove accurate or even beneficial, intuition is far more perfect. Even though most of us are not skilled in finding it, let alone using it. In Zen, this is called the beginner's mind. Understanding and unfolding your heart and mind.

There is one witch (the Wicked Witch of the West) from a movie (*The Wizard of Oz* from 1939) that still gives me nightmares. *Wicked* (the Broadway play) helps us build out the story of the Wicked Witch Elphaba. At her core, Elphaba is kind, honorable, humble, caring, independent, strong-willed, and very smart. She was just born different. Bullied, ostracized, and considered an outcast for being green. She never gets to a place or time where she feels welcomed and like she belongs. So, she builds up an abrasive and aloof exterior. Getting under that shell, Elphaba is willing to be wicked if it means she can do good. Her world turns upside down when her sister is killed by Dorothy's home falling on the Wicked Witch of the East. Elphaba personally raised her disabled sister, Nessarose Thropp. Who wouldn't turn truly wicked after that? Elphaba Thropp poignantly warns us about magicians, witches, wizards, and sorcerers: "It's people who claim that they're good … that you have to be wary of."

George Costanza (enchantingly played by Jason Alexander) is a magical character based on real-life Larry David, the writer of *Seinfeld* and the creator and star of the hilarious *Curb Your Enthusiasm*. George's flaws are many, caused by a dysfunctional childhood with odd parents. He's a liar, cheater, thief, and double-dipper who lives in his fantasy world. More official diagnoses would be a sociopath and narcissist with low self-esteem, sudden fits of anger, hypochondria, greed, selfishness, and obsessiveness. All this in a short, stocky, and balding package filled with socially awkward plots, schemes, and magic. He invented the "it's me, not you" relationship breakup routine. He concocts Vandelay Industries, a latex company. Then, there is the "puffy shirt" and George's hand modeling. He teaches physics, baseball, and hitting to Yankee icons Derek Jeter (The Captain) and Bernie Williams. Let's not forget his magic with "The Bubble Boy." Or posing on a couch in just underwear and dark dress socks. In "The Café" episode in season 3, George nails it: "You should've seen the look on her face. It was the same look my father gave me when I told him I wanted to be a ventriloquist." Wizardly.

How to Fire the Magician

I have had the pleasure of working with two larger-than-life Magicians. I have also had the distinction of giving both the unceremonious old heave-ho. The first individual was dynamic, charismatic, perceptive, and clever. They made you effortlessly feel like a close and immediate member of their family. This person's first and last names had a perfect Yoda-like ring to them. When times got tough, they would deliver a Master Yoda line out of nowhere. Something like, "Pass on what you have learned. Strength, mastery, hmm … but weakness, folly, failure, also. Yes, failure, most of all. The greatest teacher, failure is." This individual was a leadership alchemist. They were the current-day precursor to chemistry. They understood the world in all its possibilities. Their work defied all the rules. They mastered fact and intuition to turn disasters into corporate gold. Their perfect purity was the magical organizational elixir. They merged science and the spiritual to convince us there were no limits to their leadership.

Earlier in my tenure, they had a leadership hiccup. A huge one. Impacting big money, thousands of people, and the company as a whole. I overlooked all of that. I could fix it. We could find talent to replace them and fix it. We couldn't afford not to have the Magician. Arthur needed Merlin. To captivate and cultivate the organization. Wisdom, thoughtfulness, understanding, reflection, contemplation, and healing. Their "secret knowledge" would give the organization (and me as the CEO) immense power. After all, royalty always had a mage, oracle, or seer nearby. Plus, a royal psychotherapist.

I got it all wrong and wrong another time. To their credit, they were a willing ear to open up to and a comforting shoulder to lean on. They were connected to the inner and otherworldly workings of the team. And they worked some magic. But as fast as people and possibilities appeared, the Magician destroyed them. The third time is the charm, right? So, I moved them to another senior role. They made a strategic necessity that the organization had struggled with for two decades miraculously appear. Out of nowhere. I was the hero of the board and the organization. Our magic scared our competitors. They made the necessity appear, and then their magic imploded with majesty and fanfare. Completely killed the acquisition with no chance of resurrection until the end of time. Their manipulation and trickster nature caught up with them. They never lied. They just withheld. Their power to control others was enormous, but it also came without restraint. They said and did reckless things with weighty power. Underneath it all, they yearned to be king. Merlin, not Arthur. The one and only boss with all its titles and profit. This confusion turned them cold, calculating, cynical, and soulless. They never got the crown—with us, and since, for that matter.

My other Magician was full of wonder, enchantment, and excitement at all times (even when you weren't in their physical presence). They were very good-looking (almost too attractive for my jealous liking). They had already lived quite the life and were continuing to live the best life. Everything they said and did was off the hook. Their stories infused work meetings and casual gatherings with laughter or crying like you never have before. Their wide, cavernous visions of today and the future left me in awe. Another big mistake. Not with the cataclysmic consequences of the Yoda above. More like denyingly innocent and putting us into organizational quicksand. The sultry attractiveness morphed into self-indulgence and self-gratification. They, too, loved status and glory. Without the responsibility, urgency, action, and accountability to grab it. Nothing moved in their areas of responsibility. You could assign internal resources and bring in consultants to help. Help was limiting their potential and their growth. They were helpless. The miserable part of the story doesn't end there. They got a better job after losing their job with us. A first CEO job. I was even a reference, although I must admit the search consultant wasn't clear about what I was giving a reference for (and I didn't bother to ask). Within two years, they ran the same game plan, and the magic wore off. Another career change opportunity for the innocent one. Unlike their other colleague, the final chapter of this story has yet to be written. Lao-tzu, the semilegendary ancient Chinese philosopher whose text serves as the foundation of Taoism, gets this one: "He who says he knows, does not know. He who knows, does not claim to know."

Magicians appear most often in the pharmaceutical and health-care industry—as physicians, counselors in self-help circles, teachers and professors, clerics, grandparents (more likely grandfathers than grandmothers), and real-life magicians (of all things). These organizational witches and wizards won't pull out a wand. But they have the capacity to channel their energy outward with decisive aim. If someone does pull a wand on you, this book won't help.

A wand channels magical (good, bad, and the spectrum in between) energy into one place. Focused and controlled. I was part of a CEO circle in which the master facilitators had wands designed for the participants. To channel our leadership energy. Yes, there are wandmakers today. Mine was crafted by Alferian Gwydion MacLir at Bardwood, purveyors of fine druid wands. Based in Minneapolis. My wand is named *Antares* (the brightest star in the constellation of Scorpius), derived from the Ancient Greek *Ἀντάρης*, meaning "rival to Ares." The Greek god of war and courage, one of the twelve Olympians, and the son of Zeus and Hera. That fits me, right? The wand—made of walnut carved with leaves and vines with a core of spirit eagle feather, reservoir of brown tiger eye, and point of malachite—was very specific about desiring to be enchanted on the Fourth of July at sunset when all the energy of American celebration and fireworks were radiating throughout the ether. It is a physical symbol to use my inherent energy of dominance, freedom, determination, vision, truth-seeking, protection, good luck, balanced emotions, tolerance, flexibility, and openness.

Before you land in a wand battle of calamity, chaos, and confusion with your wayward wizard or witch, you must drink the spectral elixir of radical self-honesty.

Some (not even a vocal minority) of the team struggled with this at the time of the decision, while others still avoid radical self-honesty. When Magicians fail, they fail miserably because they lose all credibility. Regaining that credibility with the boss is always easier than with the team. The teams see it. They see their tricks, and they have figured them out. There is no magic. They get stuck with the consequences. And they see no other solution than the Magician magically disappearing. As the boss, this is where radical self-honesty comes in. You have to be as authentic and truthful with yourself as you are capable of being at that moment. You have to get past the parts of yourself that are easy to ignore or hide. You must work through those uncomfortable emotions and feelings to do the right thing. The Magician is all hype, marketing, and self-promotion. They have overpromised and under-delivered. Their bad decisions are now your bad decisions. Their greed, lust for power (lust to be the leader), and envy (of you and others) are their undoing. Own it.

The Least Flexible Archetype

There are excellent reasons why the Magician is the least flexible archetype to lead with when writing your fictional *New York Times* bestseller. The faults of this archetype are so consistent and predictable (read again if you missed it) that you would only have a three-chapter masterpiece. Chapter one is filled with mesmerism and amazement. Chapter two takes a 180-degree turn, with cowardice, manipulation, dishonesty, and even cultish behavior. Chapter three ends with disruption, devastation, destruction, and complete mayhem. Now, look, Magicians can return to grace. We all can. We all should experience a return to the "light." It is much more challenging for Magicians after the tricks of their craft have been exposed. Yet, I am still attracted to (and you should be, too) Magicians as part of a team, for they bring a force of healing and much-needed energy and transformation (personally, professionally, and organizationally).

TAKEAWAYS

- Be mindful of the Magician's ability to conceal their flaws as they hurtle toward inevitable disaster.
- Leaders are human too, and it is common for managers to be dazzled by the potential of this particular archetype as a team member.
- Manage the Magician's transformational energy with a firm hand.

WHAT'S NEXT

Next, we will look at the Creator, who may—or may not—be pulling their weight.

CHAPTER 14

THE CREATOR

I am, as I've said, merely competent. But, in an age of incompetence, that makes me extraordinary. –Billy Joel

THE CREATOR

The Creator is imaginative, inventive, and driven to build things of enduring meaning and value.
Think of LEGO.
Willy Wonka, but more Gene Wilder than Johnny Depp and Timothée Chalamet

The Peter Principle: Why Things Always Go Wrong was a satire written in 1969 by Laurence Peter (psychologist, educator, and hierarchiologist) and Raymond Hull (playwright and screenwriter). It's not the name of the principle that makes me a fan. Their research leading to the book is spot on. Things always go wrong. The principle is eloquent. It has fermented to this perfection in our age of incompetence. The Peter Principle is that everyone rises to their level of incompetence in a hierarchy. When you perform your job well, you are promoted. And promoted and so on. You rise up the corporate ladder until you reach the point where you can no longer perform well. The summer intern rises to CEO. From the entry-level civil servant to the country's president.

Billy Joel was right that we are living in an age of incompetence. Everyone is in control. No one is in control. Everyone has an opinion that is right. No one will talk to those who don't share that opinion. Our educational system is broken. Every year, nearly half of our children enter the school year operating below grade level in at least one subject, most often math and reading. It gets better. The National Center for Education Statistics reports that 43 percent of public school students in America attend schools where a majority of students are eligible for free or reduced-price lunch every day.[24] Just not on weekends. Our mental healthcare system is broken. More than one in five Americans live with a mental illness, while only 56 percent of them actively seek help. Two in four adults with a diagnosable condition can't access or afford the treatment they need.[25] The

24 National Center for Education Statistics, "Fast Facts: Home Schooling," accessed August 27, 2025, https://nces.ed.gov/fastfacts/display.asp?id=898.

25 National Institute of Mental Health, "Mental Illness," accessed August 27, 2025, https://www.nimh.nih.gov/health/statistics/mental-illness.

list of incompetence goes on. We have even gone to great lengths to weaponize ineptitude—dismissing the real problems, avoiding progress, and ignoring mistakes and learning opportunities. Our society today has fallen into setting the bar really low and asking for help to reach even the most basic goals.

Hierarchies reinforce bungling, and we love our hierarchies. We love working in a defined group with a clear power structure. We know it is ineffective, but it feels good. That is what really matters. Everything and everyone fits neatly in a box. In big organizations where I have worked, there are dedicated people (yes, more than one) to maintain those elaborate organizational charts. Those fancy and expensive consulting firms have developed organizational development software to help you better align those boxes, titles, and people. Those at the bottom of the organization (i.e., those who are newer and haven't been promoted) do the real work. This is where the Peter Principle slips in. The higher up you go, where the strategy, direction, and culture are developed, the more boxes are filled with the incompetent. This incompetence impacts the entire organization.

I invented the Paul Principle about twenty years ago to bolster the Peter Principle. The "Paul" isn't by accident. In a hierarchy, you can rise a level above your level of incompetence. When you perform well, you are promoted. Rinse and repeat. At some point, you will rise to a position where you can no longer perform well. At that point, despite not performing well, the company—or a competitor or another organization—will offer you another promotion two boxes above your level of competence. This is the Paul Principle. Two levels of incompetence. Whether Peter or Paul, our hierarchies, systems of hiring and promotion, operating models, organizational structures, talent management, goals, and incentives aren't serving us well. Peters and Pauls attract more Peters and Pauls to their teams. Leadership becomes snobbish and passive-aggressive (and conflict-avoidant). Listening gets shut off completely. No focus and no movement. Just more spreadsheets and reports. Jumping from one fad to another. Failures (sometimes epic), while blaming another Peter or Paul for the mistakes.

I worked with a Peter Creator archetype who turned Paul (definitely not Mary). *The* poster child for the age of incompetence. Douglas Adams best describes this leader in his 1996 triumph, *The Dilbert Principle*: "Incompetence is a natural beat of the work ecosystem. Embrace it, and you'll have job security for life."[26] They were a long-termer in the organization. Rising from intern to one of the top three senior leaders by title. A few in the organization lauded them as Mensa intelligent. I didn't buy it. It was a matter of perspective. Set the bar low (like really low), and everyone can be a genius. To give them props, they were highly creative, imaginative, and visionary. They gave you the feeling of innovation and invention. When you probed, you, unfortunately, found someone who didn't know much about their paid role, and they knew absolutely nothing about anything outside of that role (despite working in the industry for decades). Their "inventiveness" was narrowly focused, overly idealistic, and not practical. Their designs had no place in the real world. Being highly imaginative, they developed a strong personal sense of aesthetic—beauty, emotion, sensation, and good taste framed in their unique point of view. We ended up with an interior decorator, architect, and engineer (literally playing those roles in the organization as well as an artist, inventor, musician, writer, and mad scientist). Poorly, I might add, along with solutions that were not reliable or viable. What we really needed (and

26 Scott Adams, *The Dilbert Principle: A Cubicle's-Eye View of Bosses, Meetings, Management Fads & Other Workplace Afflictions* (Harper Business, 1996).

what they were being paid handsomely to do) was to be a math wizard, keen analyst, strategic thinker, risk manager, and ethical leader.

Should we talk about the ethical leader? If there was an *-ist* to label them as, they earned every one of them. We could add another chapter to the Lover archetype just for this leader and their innate scorn for anyone not like them. The good news is that they didn't discriminate in how they discriminated. Direct. Indirect. Harassment. Victimization. And so much more. If you could overlook that behavior, you found they weren't reliable or consistent. Their work product was amateur. They undermined and backstabbed. They were deceitful and lacked truthfulness. A bad liar at that. And utterly devoid of self-awareness. A negative seven on a scale of one to ten. This person wasn't coachable by me, their executive coach, or anyone else. You can't coach those who completely lack self-awareness. It is their world, not the real world. For reasons I won't elaborate here, you couldn't streamline this person out of the organization.

The only option was to minimize their impact on others. Do their work for them (that included me). Move their office away from others to avoid damage. Diminish those who reported to them. The fewer people and projects they were around, the better we performed. We made our Creator visibly and definitively unimportant and insignificant (and, not in a nice way, undervalued and unheard).

Dr. Victor Frankenstein from Mary Shelley's 1818 novel, *Frankenstein; or, The Modern Prometheus* is akin to the Creator archetype. Dr. Frankenstein has a curious mind and a passionate interest in advancing scientific development. However, his ambition, arrogance, insolence, and single-mindedness lead him to see himself as a god who creates life itself. The failed experiment humbles him, to say the least. Victor dies wishing he could destroy the monster he created. Come to think of it, maybe more like Dr. Frederick Frankenstein, played magnificently by Gene Wilder, in Mel Brooks's 1974 *Young Frankenstein*. Frederick, a lecturing brain surgeon who commits his life to teaching and taking care of the living, inherits his infamous grandfather's (Dr. Victor) castle on top of a hill in Transylvania. He discovers *How I Did It* in the estate's private library and can't think of anything other than honoring his family by doing it again. Make the dead alive. Supported by Igor (played by Marty Feldman, the architect of British comedy), the grandson of Victor's Igor, Inga (played by Teri Garr, with over 140 television and movie credits), and Elizabeth Lavenza (played by Madeline Kahn, a trailblazing comedienne), his intellectual, passionate, driven, eccentric, and quite possibly insane nature plays out the story according to history.

A simpler example would be Jennifer Aniston as Rachel Green in *Friends*. One of Rachel's most positive qualities is her sense of style. She works in the fashion industry after all (with Fortunata Fashions, Bloomingdale's, and Ralph Lauren) and enjoys shopping and keeping up with the latest style trends. Rachel is caring, but then again, every character on this ten-season, sixty-two-time Primetime Emmy–nominated (only six wins) show appears to be kind. She is beautiful, successful, engaging, charming, and fun. And quick-witted, delightfully sarcastic, snappy, and memorable. Rachel intensely believes in finding true love, which drives her unwavering loyalty. She is the one out of the six you most want to hang out with. Yet, she is flawed, like all Creator types. She is spoiled. Growing up, she had everything money could buy, including popularity. Attractive and stylish, yet also somewhat vain, entitled, and selfish. Occasionally deceitful. Avoiding confrontation and not great at being assertive.

Creators Gone Bad

It would be best if you had Creators in organizations that pride themselves on innovation, companies that highly value self-expression, or brands whose outputs are artistic and "do-it-yourself" products or services. You can use creative leaders in fields such as architecture, business development, marketing, communications, public relations, the arts, and maybe even interior design. Creators create. Both the tangible and the intangible.

When things aren't going well, you will get tangled in a lot of lofty ideals. A singular focus to their efforts, and that is their focus (not yours or the organization's). Nothing practical or usable sees the light of day. When that annual assessment time comes, you will be hard-pressed to find any (literally any) accomplishments. The Creator neglects the real world (while they are living in their own world), and, as a result, they neglect everyone around them (direct reports, peers, teams, and you as the boss). Chronic procrastination is their art. Perfectionism is their science. Perfect is the enemy of good. In the original Italian, it is, "*Il meglio è l'inimico del bene*" (the best is the enemy of the good) from the *Dictionnaire Philosophique* written in 1764 by François-Marie Arouet, known by his nom de plume, Voltaire—a French Enlightenment philosopher and historian known for his sharp wit and sharper criticism. At the same time, you have to answer to Jim Collins's *Good to Great*: "I'd like to start with a challenge: Good is the enemy of great. Good is the mortal enemy of great. If you think about it, it's one of the main reasons why we have so few things that become truly great."

If your company doesn't value creativity, it doesn't have creatives running around. If your Creator is struggling, find the right person who can paint and sing for you. Otherwise, cut your losses and help them find a place to practice their art. If you can't cut them loose, freeze them out and minimize their ability to cause you to lose sleep (mainly from having to get up early and stay up late doing their work).

TAKEAWAYS

- Ensure that your organization needs a Creator before hiring one.
- Be mindful of Creators who are stuck in the perfectionism trap.
- If Creators can't be exited, minimize their damage and scope until they can.

WHAT'S NEXT

Next, and finally, we are going to look at the Sage.

CHAPTER 15

THE SAGE

The harder you work, the harder it is to surrender. –Vince Lombardi

THE SAGE

The Sage is deeply committed to helping the world gain deeper insight and wisdom, serving as a thoughtful mentor and advisor.
Think PBS television.
Wax on, wax off with Mr. Miyagi.

The Sage embodies the personification of wisdom and knowledge. You will find the Sage brand used in schools, universities, consulting firms, media networks, and search engines. Classic Sages in our everyday consciousness include Albert Einstein, Stephen Hawking, Jane Goodall, and the Dalai Lama. And we can't possibly exclude Oprah Winfrey. Who isn't enamored with lively, social, supportive, ambitious, driven, focused, bold, strong, confident, and determined people? Albus Dumbledore from J. K. Rowling's *Harry Potter* series is the quintessential Sage character in literature, offering the protagonist guidance and wisdom. Wise, intelligent, mysterious in his own way, gentle, caring, and understanding. Mentor and protector for Harry and the driving force for the young wizard to be more brilliant, brave, and caring.

One of the great Sages of our times is unquestionably the wunderkind Texan who started college at the age of eleven and received his first doctorate at the age of sixteen. Dr. Sheldon Cooper from *The Big Bang Theory* (played by Jim Parsons) and *Young Sheldon* (played by Iain Armitage). He is a superiorly intelligent geek who speaks Klingon, wears superhero T-shirts, and, indeed, knows everything about everything. He loves routine and hygiene. His understanding of irony, sarcasm, humor, humility, and empathy is tenuous at best. Dr. Cooper, forever the Sage, says, "I always listen to myself. It's one of the great joys of my life."

Perhaps the most controversial Sage in our era is Richard Bruce "Dick" Cheney, the forty-sixth vice president of the United States from 2001 to 2009 under President George W. Bush. He served as chief of staff under President Gerald Ford, secretary of defense under President H. W. Bush, and was in the House of Representatives for a decade, serving the people of Wyoming. President Bush called him "Big Time." Those around him would personally describe him as mild and private.

An individualist to a fault, hardworking, willing to help a neighbor, a lover of the land, and hardheaded. He doesn't talk unless he has to. When he does speak, he is brisk and uses phrases (not sentences), yet you always get the sense that he understands the full and complete picture. The strong but silent type. It's a Wyoming stereotype. His public persona, on the other hand, is dark. It is said that George Lucas based the character of Darth Plagueis (who could cheat death and create life and was the mentor of Emperor Palpatine/Darth Sidious, who betrayed Plagueis and murdered him in his sleep) on Cheney. He is painted publicly as a power-hungry capitalist, seizing control and running a personal agenda, seizing on the turmoil of the 9/11 attacks, the war on terror, and the collapse of the Soviet Union. Regardless of which side you sit on, Vice President Cheney was a Washington Sage and truth-teller who remained passionate about our democracy.

I bumped into "Vice" in the hallway of the hospital I was operationally leading after a quail hunting accident in South Texas in 2006. It was a strange set of events that were expected, confusing, and surreal all at the same time. I was stuck behind a door watching the vice president enter, briefly stay, and then fly out of the trauma intensive care unit (ICU). That dichotomy of private and dark on full display. After his visit on a Sunday morning, I went into the ICU to meet the individual hurt in the accident and talk to the staff. A seasoned nurse came up to me and said, "Cheney shot that guy." I blew her comments off. "I have worked here for twenty-five years. He had shooter's eyes," the nurse said. In that bemusing conversation, my pager went off. It was my wife. She told me that the media was reporting that the vice president had shot someone while hunting the day before. Yeah, maybe. At least this expert nurse thought so. Pulling into work early the next morning, I found every news station on the planet lined up on the street outside the hospital. Cheney did it. Big time. And then came my fifteen minutes of fame. I spent the next week doing international news conferences with a trusty emergency medicine physician at my side and enjoyed a direct line to the White House. No need for six degrees of separation to the most powerful vice president and, at the same time, one of the most loathed political figures in our country's history.

Unlike for Dr. Cooper and Vice President Cheney, time isn't always a blessing. You can stay too long in one place. I worked with one of those Sage leaders. It had been time (for quite some time) for them and the organization to move on. For the health and success of both. The individual's career had skyrocketed in the organization to a key senior-level position and the key advisor to the previous CEO. They had worked for multiple CEOs, which is a significant accomplishment in and of itself. They navigated internal and external politics adeptly. Brought wisdom, strategic thinking, and context to the organization and its conversations. I appreciated their wild sense of both energy and emotion. Guided by truth and logic, their stoic character made them stand out in the leadership crowd. Their mind was their most prized possession, and they were always full of insights to share. Typical of the Sage archetype, this leader also came off as cold, critical, isolated, and overly cautious. Not intentional. Not negative. But still very visible to old-timers and newcomers alike. When you have been around a long time, those things don't sit well, and they eventually come home to roost. When things got painfully apparent—except to the Sage—we did a 360-degree assessment. It was painfully blunt and bluntly ugly. The Sage finally saw it. It made this departure easy for everyone. I am happy to see them thriving in a new organization and in a new role where they are welcome but aren't able to wear out their welcome anytime soon.

Then, there was the individual who stayed too long in the organization, retired in place, and refused to leave without a fight. They were the third generation of a family that had worked in and around the organization for just about a century of service. Dumbledore was around 115 or 116 at the time of his death. This one sits in the witch/wizard resilience category. I found them immediately wise, assuring, knowledgeable, influential, reliable, and factual. With all the history, expertise, and credibility to back it up. Unfortunately, time made them painfully cynical, overly cautious, unsympathetic, and restless. This leader turned passive to the point where they would not act on anything. And they were perfectly comfortable with others on the team (including me as CEO) doing their work for them. Even the most basic tasks. To make it worse, they pawned things off in an arrogant and holier-than-thou manner. The team finally marched into my office as a group and gave me their ultimatum—take action with the Sage, or they would leave the organization one by one. I made the change. I offered a soft landing. We addressed any financial issues related to retirement. In response, they viewed it all as a violation of their service and that of their entire family. They left the organization with a smile but retreated to their ivory tower to launch a dogmatic and emotionless crusade to remove me from my position. They were right. They were wronged. They tried to leverage their hard-won wisdom and credibility earned over decades. A small crowd of other fired leaders joined the cause. Their closest allies abandoned them.

I've seen this next sad example time and time again. The model Sage. This person hired me to replace them as CEO, as they sought retirement in a year or less. I had known them for over a decade. They had hired me before. They talked about retiring all the time. What they wanted to do. How they wanted to live. They were part guru—naturally intelligent and knowledgeable. Part Aristotle—reflective, deep thinking, and a creator of clarity. I considered them a mentor who taught me the value of thinking things through and motivating the team to seek the truth. They were also the investigator (researching and gathering hordes of information) and the analyst (excited and challenged by understanding deep problems). You would routinely get a treasure of an email on a weekend that furthered your understanding of the issue you might be ignoring and gave you direction on where to go and what to do by Monday morning. When it came time to announce their retirement, it was crickets. When I asked, I wasn't ready to take over. They were ready for me to take over. It was governance that had the issues. That was not what was going on. They were not ready to retire. The board eventually worked with them to keep their retirement right on schedule. The caveat was that they needed to stay on for a year in an advisory capacity to mentor me and work on two initiatives. OK, they were not retiring. Their two pet projects were an obsession to the exclusion of everything else. Fixated and rigid. Their way or the highway. However, things were changing. What they had built for a decade was changing or going away. There was a new sheriff in town. No room for two CEOs. It was an irritating year for me. And for them. We haven't talked since.

I remember my grandparents greatly looking forward to retirement. It was an expectation. It was a time-honored tradition. There were parties, great gifts, and a chance to tour the world (or the country or the town). Recent surveys showed that 17 percent of Americans want to retire before the golden age of sixty-five. Unfortunately, in the same surveys, 29 percent of Americans under fifty-five don't think they will ever be able to afford to retire. Surveys also show that 78 percent of Americans live paycheck to paycheck. And that number is increasing. More than three in four, and it's not just who you think. Why do you think the 2011 NFL lockout only lasted 132 days? The average union strike in our country only lasts forty days.[27] The most recent autoworker strike lasted forty-six days (three paychecks).

If you can financially retire, other things get in the way of actually setting the date and sticking to it. Most of us never really put our thinking into it. It seems so far away. But it creeps up on us. So many people have nothing to retire to. My grandfather spent sixteen years in the United States Army and more than three decades working at a chemical company. He gave up many a holiday with his family to "union bust" for the company across the country. Yet, they forced his retirement when they thought he wasn't needed anymore. He spent the rest of his almost twenty years sitting in his favorite chair and not doing much else. For leaders, especially senior leaders and even more so CEOs, it is a loss of power. No more power lunches or dinners. No more assistants managing your day. No more perks. No more texts or emails flying to you to make a decision. You don't have to make any decisions at all anymore. Except maybe when to get out of the chair for meals. For everyone, retirement means losing what we love to do. We begin working at eighteen or twenty-two or maybe even fifteen, like my grandfather, and devote our lives to one cause for the next forty years. We spend more time at work than with our families and friends. Then, one day, it is all over.

There is one leader with whom I worked who put a lot of thought into retirement. I never understood why he would make personal financial decisions based on speeding up his retirement. Come raise and bonus time, he would whip out a neatly designed spreadsheet and calculate his new retirement date. If it went in the wrong direction, you wanted to stay away from him for the next month. An opportunity

---

27 Stephan Bisaha et al., "The Never-Ending Strike," NPR, January 5, 2023, https://www.npr.org/2023/01/05/1147120215/the-never-ending-strike.

presented itself to move up retirement by two years, and he took the offer. He had so much more yet to give. I called him after six months into retirement and offered him an interim opportunity with my team. He told me never to call him with an offer again. He was retired. Day trading now. He had lost weight. He was off a slew of medications. He had never felt better in his life. He loved retirement. That made me love the thought of retirement. It changed my thinking.

When I was interning with a CEO during the summer in graduate school, he told me one day at lunch that I would know when it was time to leave an organization. I wanted to say, "I am twenty-four. I want to get through this summer. And get a great job with a great title, paying lots of money, when I get that Ivy League degree. Why would I ever be thinking about leaving?" I know I did a spectacular job during the internship, but the CEO didn't offer me a full-time job after graduation, maybe because I blew off his message about leaving. What he knew and I didn't at twenty-four is that we all turn into the Sage or some version of it.

Don't Be the Sage

Please don't find yourself in the position of the Sage in the organization and stay too long. Also, I can't stress this one enough: Please, please, please don't find yourself in the position of the Sage in the organization and they ask you to retire. You need to retire according to your timeline and terms. First and foremost, you must ensure you are financially secure for your retirement. Do you find yourself thinking about retirement? Are you satisfied with your work and what you have accomplished? Does your family support you in deciding to retire? Do you feel like you have more to give the world than what you are doing right now? Are you indeed ready to do something new? To meet new people and develop new relationships? Choosing to retire is a huge decision. When you get to a place where you answer these questions affirmatively, it is time to write the next chapters in your story.

Dealing with the Sage

Don't let your Sage leader stay too long, retire in place, not fully retire, or retire discourteously. It isn't healthy for them. It isn't healthy for you or the organization. The Sage deserves more. Don't let it get to the point where their fantasies become your realities. Don't let them manipulate you, the team, or the organization. Cut their cult following off at the pass. Don't let this devolve into money and power struggles. Sit down with them in person. Be completely transparent about the decision. As direct as possible. The natural and personal truth is that it is time. Rise above their attempts to contradict and stand above you. Show that you value their many contributions over the years. Take money off the table for them. Express your gratitude, thanks, support, and confidence in the departing Sage. Never a bad word (despite what their actions may cause you to want to do). Always their accomplishments. Never ever their failures or faults.

The Timeline

A transition timeline is essential when taking a leadership role or transitioning out of one. Some will tell you that ninety days works well. I've had a year transitioning with a CEO. I have had thirty days. I have had a CEO leave six months before my arrival without a transition.

It's not good or bad. It just is. You have to do what is suitable for the organization. Not the two of you. The right amount of time could be none, a few hours, days, or even weeks. I personally don't suggest anything beyond thirty days. Leadership transitions are inherently not smooth. So, please don't do anything to make it worse.

Be firm and clear when the exiting leader will leave, especially if that exiting leader is you. Once you announce you are going, you are a lame duck. Don't make decisions that the next person will have to live with. Hand it over gracefully. Like an Olympic track relay, ensure the next leader has the baton. They may not grab it like you did. They may run faster or slower than you did. Not your problem. You ran your race and handed it off successfully. Exit gracefully. Embrace your next chapter. Your next chapter is not the next leader's chapter. You are writing different books. You may never talk to your replacement ever again. You definitely won't be best friends. Don't sweat it.

When You Follow a Sage

I have followed wildly successful CEOs (you want to be the person to follow the person who follows the hall-of-fame CEO) and ones who left complete and utter messes (more of that because the successful CEOs usually have an internal replacement). Regardless of the person who came before you, always honor them. This may take so much tongue biting that you will be bleeding 24/7 for the first few months. Grin and bear it. Spend too much time (at least the first ninety to one hundred days) listening, observing, and learning. Know what your predecessor did well. Understand the legacy, history, DNA, and context of the organization. Get into the details. You can't afford to hover at fifty thousand feet out of the gate. Gather and consolidate that comprehensive understanding of your new organization and role. Use that to craft a clear road map for the future. Balancing change for change's sake with imperatives and essentiality. Use this as an opportunity to get everyone (or most) to buy in. Share it with the team, board, and anyone else who will listen. Put yourself into the position of being the best possible Sage for your new role and team.

If all else fails in your journey with the Sage leader and transitions in leadership, burn some sage. Indigenous peoples created the practice of "saging" to purify spaces, lift spirits, rid areas of negative energy, and promote healing and wisdom. A study documented that burning white prairie sage (also known as estafiate, which grows wild throughout North America) or taking a sage-infused bath creates the balance necessary to deal with the failed Sage on your team. Also, not a bad way to help with confusion about your own transitions and retirement.

TAKEAWAYS

- Don't let Sages overstay their welcome.
- Handle the transition with dignity and directness.
- If you are following a Sage, learn and observe first.

WHAT'S NEXT

By now, you're well acquainted with the various archetypes in your company. Next, I want to talk about you.

CHAPTER 16

BE KIND, NOT NICE

Love isn't a perfect state of caring. It's an active noun, like "struggle." –Fred Rogers

You got the tough part for fifteen chapters. Now you get heart. When I say *heart,* I don't mean *nice.* You never want to be called "nice" in a personal relationship. The adage is that nice locks you in the friend zone. You also don't want to be nice in leadership. Nice is often expressed through words and gestures. That is where it falls short. Nice hurts healthy and open communication. It puts aside your wants and needs for those of all others. It lays all the responsibility for someone else's behavior on you while getting them off the hook entirely and avoiding your own responsibilities in the process. Nice builds resentment and frustration. I've never been called nice. In fact, the direct opposite. Successful leaders want to be called something completely different.

Be kind. One of the earliest known uses of the word *kindness* is in the Middle English period (from 1150 to 1550). It was generally used to mean *wellborn* or *well-bred.* Born out of those roots, it has evolved to mean a giving nature. Doing good deeds for others. To be kind is to be charitable, helpful, and eager to assist. Good deeds for yourself, others, and the world around us. Words, gestures, and, most importantly, actions. Not just a noun or adjective but an action verb.

The best way I have found to describe how to be kind is another word: *compassion. Compassion* comes from the ancient Greek *συμπάθεια* [sympatheia], meaning fellow feeling. And also *σπλαγχνίζομαι* [splagchnizomai], which means the stirring of the inward parts, literally the twisting of the intestines. In the "Parable of the Prodigal Son" found in the Gospel of Luke in the Bible, *splagchnizomai* is the exact word used by the narrator. Father Donald P. McNeill, a member of the Congregation of the Holy Cross, and Father Henri J. M. Nouwen, a priest in the Archdiocese of Utrecht (Netherlands) (with two other authors) wrote *Compassion: A Reflection on the Christian Life* in 1982. I took a theology class in my senior year led by the late Father Don with his guest, Father Nouwen, an international legend in spirituality, psychology, social justice, community, and pastoral ministry. My favorite memory from Theology and Community Service was Nouwen's authentic and practical take on the Prodigal Son. Five years later, after our brief time together, he published *The Return of the Prodigal Son: A Story of Homecoming.* I was twenty-one and didn't even remotely appreciate who had been teaching that class. I skimmed the book as necessary during the semester. Today, I always keep it right next to my phone on my desk.

Now, consider these eloquent sentences from the book *Compassion*: "Are we really servants when we can become masters again once we think we have done our part or made our contribution? Are we really servants when we can say when, where, and how long we will give of our time and energy? Is service in a far country really an expression of servanthood when we keep enough money in the bank to fly home at any moment?"[28]

These influences have been so impactful to my calling that my wife Liz and I are actively involved today in the Center for Social Concerns at Notre Dame (founded by McNeill in 1983), where I took that formative class in 1989. *Compassion* isn't just Christian or Catholic. It is the way to think about leadership. In service to others. In community. With displacement and reflection. In action.

Why Servant Leadership Is Essential

The primary lens through which we view life, leadership, and business is competition. There are waiting lists to get into the "best" daycare centers and kindergartens. We take standardized tests every year and get classified by ranks and percentiles. I clearly remember the Mother Superior visiting my Catholic elementary school and telling me I would never get into Notre Dame because I wasn't reading well. In the first grade! I told her my coloring was exceptional with the Crayola sixty-four pack. Private, preparatory, and specialized high schools. Advanced Placement classes to earn college credit. SATs and ACTs. College advisors. MCATs, LSATs, GREs, and GMATs. Who runs the fastest? Who eats the most hot dogs on the Fourth of July? More and bigger and better.

Competition is critical. We compete in the products and services we offer to our customers. We compete in our supply chains for the highest-quality inputs. We compete for talent to drive everything we

28 Donald P. McNeill et al., *Compassion: A Reflection on the Christian Life* (Image Books, 1982).

do. Business is more competitive than ever before. Today, the average lifespan of a company on the S&P 500 Index is just over twenty-one years, compared with thirty-two years in 1965.[29] I once had a competitor CEO publicly state that their sole mission was to put my company (which was originally established in 1875) out of business. Good luck with that strategy. President Theodore Roosevelt, of Rough Rider and "walk softly and carry a big stick" fame, cautioned: "Comparison is the thief of joy."

A competitive spirit is essential. Don't get me wrong here. Professionalism is good. Being the best and more than competent helps. Setting goals and persevering to achieve them. Showing flexibility with accountability and responsibility. Exceeding expectations. Doing whatever it takes. Finding innovative solutions to old problems and new situations. We all want to work in competitive organizations. The famous rental car company Avis, with its slogan "We Try Harder," falls short. Winning feels good.

Competition becomes unhealthy when it turns into control. When you think that your success comes at the expense of others. When it is based on scarcity and fear. When it takes over your thoughts, you put too much pressure on yourself and all those around you. You start neglecting the crucial things. The ones you love and the ones you need (especially at work). A cutthroat and no-matter-what-it-takes attitude is about you winning, not the team, organization, or community winning.

Control is an illusion. It is a lack of self-awareness. It needs the ingredient of understanding your place in the world. You don't own the organization. In most cases, you didn't start it. In all cases, you

---

29 D. Clark, "Average Company Lifespan of S&P 500 Companies 1965–2030," Statista, June 26, 2025, https://www.statista.com/statistics/1259275/average-company-lifespan/.

aren't going to finish (or so we all hope). You are put in your position for a spot in time. The average lifespan of today's multinational, *Fortune* 500-sized corporation is roughly fifty years (average revenue size of $42 billion with almost seventy thousand employees).[30] I've had the pleasure of leading healthcare organizations founded in the late 1800s. I've had the misfortune of ending an organization. Male *Fortune* 500 CEOs ran their firms for an average of 7.2 years. Sadly, the average tenure for female CEOs was only 4.5 years.[31] That is the next book. So, as a CEO, you are only at the helm of your global company for less than 15 percent of the company's total existence. You stand on the shoulders of the giants who came before you. You are entrusted with history and people to carry forward to the next CEO and the next generation.

With the publication of *Servant Leadership* in 1977, Robert K. Greenleaf, a retired AT&T executive, ushered in the modern era of servant leadership. While servant leadership is a timeless biblical concept, Greenleaf, in his 1970 essay *The Servant as Leader*, said, "The servant-leader is servant first … It begins with the natural feeling that one wants to serve, to serve first. Then conscious choice brings one to aspire to lead. That person is sharply different from one who is a leader first, perhaps because of the need to assuage an unusual power drive or to acquire material possessions … The leader-first and the

30 Mark Goodburn, "What Is the Life Expectancy of Your Company?" World Economic Forum, January 24, 2015, https://www.weforum.org/stories/2015/01/what-is-the-life-expectancy-of-your-company/.

31 Lila MacLellan, "It's Not Your Imagination. Women CEOs at Fortune 500 Companies Really Do Have Shorter Tenures Than Men," *Fortune*, February 20, 2024, https://fortune.com/2024/02/20/women-ceos-fortune-500-shorter-tenure-men/.

servant-first are two extreme types. Between them, there are shadings and blends that are part of the infinite variety of human nature."[32]

The Four Characteristics

Servant leadership is still more of a topic of books, blogs, live streams, and speeches than it is put into everyday use. Servant-first leaders have four key characteristics: *listening*, *empathy*, *flexibility*, and *stewardship*. These four are encircled by awareness, healing, foresight, conceptualization, persuasion, commitment to the growth of others, and community building. The servant-leader's kindness, patience, and understanding are what our business world (and moving people out of our organizations) needs to cure what ails us. It is a place where influence and support rule. These leaders care about their individuals and their teams. They care about their organizations. And the organizations' place in the community, in the world, in the environment, in social justice, in sustainability, and with all stakeholders. This is legitimate control, competitiveness, and power.

Find Your Leadership Tribe

Tribes became our predominant form of society between thirty thousand and thirty-five thousand years ago. The planet was in the grip of an ice age. Communities were formed to share food, care for infants and children, and divide labor to meet the daily challenges

32 Robert K. Greenleaf, *Servant Leadership: A Journey into the Nature of Legitimate Power and Greatness* (Paulist Press, 1977).

of that environment. Darwin and survival of the fittest stuff. Also, let's acknowledge that humans are social animals and are entirely ill-equipped to live independently. Commitment to a group, kinship, a sense of identity, and a fulfilled need for belonging are the essential elements of culture, tribes, and society.

Catholic religious communities emerged as early as 529 AD with the Order of St. Benedict. Benedict of Nursia, a sixth-century Italian monk, laid the foundations of Benedictine monasticism through the formation of Saint Benedict's Rule—an organized day with regular private and community prayer, sleep, spiritual reading, and manual labor. The Benedictines grew into a confederation of independent abbeys and priories unified through one leadership structure. The first kibbutz (from the Hebrew word *kvutza*, meaning "group") was established over ninety years ago. It was a revolutionary idea whereby people would commit, in a voluntary society, to a living and working contract based on egalitarian, communal, social, and economic principles. Kibbutzim are known for their strong sense of community, with residents sharing resources and working together to achieve common goals.

Estimates from the Inter-American Commission on Human Rights in the United Nations and the nonprofit group Survival International are that there are between one hundred and two hundred uncontacted tribes on our planet, numbering up to ten thousand people in aggregate.[33] These are groups of Indigenous peoples living without sustained contact with our world. No cell phones. No cable television. No electric vehicles. No airports. No space travel. No leadership books. The Sentinelese are the most isolated tribe on earth,

33 "Uncontacted Tribes," Survival International, accessed August 26, 2025, https://www.survivalinternational.org/campaigns/uncontacted.

living only on North Sentinel Island (part of India). Most estimates number this tribe as low as fifteen members to as many as two hundred. They hunt wild boar and use single-outrigger canoes for fishing and turtle hunting. They sleep on the ground, not on raised platforms or beds. Their clothing is sparse, with only a few necklaces, headbands, and jewelry. The Indian government does not allow travel to the island. The Sentinelese discourage all visitors with arrows. From a safe distance, the Sentinelese are healthy and thriving to this day.

We can't ignore the compelling argument that leadership is also a team sport. Robustness and prosperity demand that we work as a tribe. To be kind, we must find our tribe, make authentic connections, and work with people who love and support us.

Get Comfortable Being Uncomfortable

Ian Lancaster Fleming, best known for his James Bond series of spy novels, advised that "A horse is dangerous at both ends and uncomfortable in the middle." Our lives have become too comfortable. Too many leaders wallow in their comfort zones all the time. However, growth thrives in discomfort. Researchers at the Carnegie Institution for Science have reported that the formation of Earth was much more chaotic than previously thought.[34] They have found evidence within the rocks of volcanic hot spots that reveals disorderly behavior during the planet's formative years. Order comes from chaos. So, too, our comfort comes from a place of discomfort. A zone where we take the unfamiliar, challenging, and uncertain into our hearts.

---

34 Colin R. M. Jackson et al., "Early Episodes of High-Pressure Core Formation Preserved in Plume Mantle," *Nature* 553, no. 7689 (2018): 491–495, https://doi.org/10.1038/nature25446.

Irish teacher and poet John O'Donohue captured this place of discomfort so well in *To Bless the Space Between Us: A Book of Blessings.* "Teacher" and "poet" don't quite fit the late O'Donohue. An elegant and thought-filled author, Celtic spiritualist, Hegelian philosopher, and former priest. A role model of prayer, meditation, caring for others, and being one with nature. The space between us is that uncomfortable space. Life's great thresholds . . . such as getting married, having children, starting a new job, birthdays, old age, death, homecoming, and addiction. Transitioning from the known and familiar into the new and unmapped. His poems and blessings offer us the opportunity to awaken to timeless truths and demonstrate our power to navigate through periods of change and transition. Finding comfort in the uncomfortable.

Compassion calls this principle "displacement." Leading away from the ordinary and proper. We get to cast off our illusions of control and the facade we put on that we have it all together. Not settling into a false sense of comfort. This leads to having crucial conversations with ourselves about the most profound questions. What is our reason for being? What is our understanding of who we are in relation to those around us? Our friends and family? Our work tribe? Our neighbors and community? Our world? Our universe? All the while recognizing that we are not alone on this road. All humans are in a fundamentally unsettled position shared with all other humans. With the possibility of bringing us together in fathomless solidarity.

Be Relentlessly Patient

I am still working on this one. I've been working on it for at least two decades. OK, my whole life. I have that surgeon mentality. If it doesn't work, cut it out. Patience is a lost art. Our world has become too fast-paced. We crave instant gratification, but patience is good for us (me, too). Patience enables self-control, self-love, and self-care. It reduces stress, lowers heart rate, and improves physical health. Patience leads to more happiness in leadership and in the workplace.

Patience is one of the seven heavenly virtues (along with temperance, charity, chastity, humility, diligence, and, yes, kindness), dating back to *Psychomachia*, a poem written by the late-antique Latin poet Prudentius in the early fifth century AD. Seven deadly sins and seven heavenly virtues. Not a coincidence. Patience is not natural. It is a practical skill that can be developed. We can practice it. Starting with small things builds our capabilities to apply patience when dealing with medium, large, and massive things. In that practice, be in the moment. Be in your mind, your heart, and your soul. Get in touch with yourself. Change your perspective on what sits in front of you. Change conversations. Explore all the options and alternatives. Accept that all the things in the situation are things that you cannot control. Remember what matters most. Finally, be kind to yourself.

If you are still struggling with patience and maybe even find it impossible to master, let me tell you a bit about the Tendai Lotus School, a Mahāyāna Buddhist tradition, and the Tendai monks of Mount Hiei near Kyoto. Have you ever thought about running a marathon? Nope. Have you run a marathon? How many? How about one marathon per day for one hundred days? How about one marathon per day for one hundred days each year for seven years? Oh, yeah, running in straw sandals. Praying the entire way. After all that running, you go into a darkened room for nine days without food, water, or sleep. This practice is called *kaihōgyō* (translated to "circling the mountain"). The idea behind this grueling and ceaseless movement is to exhaust the mind, the body, and everything. If you pull off this practice of ultimate patience, you are literally a human Buddha. And achieve the title of *dai-ajari* … yes, a living Buddha.

Reflect and Discern

Patience is furthered and honed by formal reflection. Many fields—education, nursing, social work, and psychology, to name just a few—formally employ reflective practice. Reflection for an educator might look like teacher self-assessment, classroom observations, student evaluations, or detailed educational research. Reflection for an athlete might look like thinking about mistakes made during a training session (watching film, meeting with coaches, talking to teammates, and just being with yourself) and figuring out how to avoid repeating those mistakes (especially in game situations).

Patience is furthered by discernment. Some organizations have formal discernment processes for major corporate decisions. Typically, faith-based or strongly mission-driven organizations. It is relatively rare, even in churches. Trained facilitators help guide the process, the leader, and the team. Ascension Health, a healthcare network of more than 140 hospitals and 140,000 team members across twenty states, employs the Christian practice of discernment with a seven-step process:

1. Identify the central question.
2. Consider stakeholders.
3. Identify the relevant facts.
4. Identify salient values and moral concerns.
5. Consider alternatives.

6. Decide and justify.
7. Follow up and review.

Reflective practice and discernment—both formal and informal—should ideally involve all of the following:

- Being intentional and deliberate about contemplation requires allocating the right amount of time. This may take hours, months, or even a year or more. It depends on the people, context, past, present, future, stakeholders, and perspectives.
- Assess yourself and the situation. Tell yourself the truth. Honestly and accurately measure performance.
- Think critically. Question everything. The real, perceived, and rumored. Not just "what" but also "why." So what? Now what?
- Challenge yourself and the situation. Lay out all the possibilities and potential paths. Tally the positives and negatives. What's next?
- Choose the path—the path for change, how to communicate, whom to engage, how to act, and what plan to execute.
- Evaluate new learnings. What worked well? What didn't work so well? What would you stop, start, and keep? These questions are intended to inform your next reflection and discernment more fully.

Be Actively Kind

Kindness is an action verb. Kindness without action is just powerless faith. It's that *nice* word again. Without action, you give up all your power. Without action, you rely on someone else to make things up. Remember the root of compassion: "to suffer with." Awareness alone is not enough. To suffer with, the awareness must permeate our entire being. We must deeply, intensely, inwardly, and outwardly feel the suffering, injustice, or the problem. We have to be touched by it. Kindness and compassion require action.

One of your team members crossed the line related to DEI (in both words and actions). Are you going to say something about it? What are you going to do about it? Governance and leadership have the platitude that "our people come first." But come annual raise time, they chose to skip it this year. They avoided making the tough decisions to improve financial performance. So, everyone suffers. Wait; leadership will still get their bonuses. Are you going to say something about it? What are you going to do about it?

The CEO and CFO are misstating the financial statements. The auditors are looking the other way. Only you know all the details. Are you going to say something about it? What are you going to do about it?

The quality of our new product is, at best, a "C." There are safety concerns that consumers could be harmed. Are you going to say something about it? What are you going to do about it?

These aren't just hypothetical situations. Accounting and financial scandals abound. Bernie Madoff. Lehman Brothers. Freddie Mac. Enron. Product launches too. New Coke. The Ford Edsel. McDonald's Arch Deluxe. Apple's Newton. Google Lively. And product failures. They knew, and they failed to act. And people were hurt. Seriously and fatally. Easy-Bake Oven. Vioxx. Toyota's gas pedals. Tylenol poisonings. 737 MAX. Bean bag chairs. Baby slings. High chairs. These are epic governance and leadership failures. And they keep happening. They might even be happening in your organization (or mine) right now.

Leaders are paid to execute. There is a cost to this. Put aside your self-interests and what is easy. Put the cause at hand ahead of yourself. Make the hard decision for the team. Not the safe decision. Make the change that is so long overdue. Take action. Today. Lawrence Bossidy and Ram Charan wrote in the classic *Execution: The Discipline of Getting Things Done*: "Execution is a systematic process of rigorously discussing how's and what's, questioning, tenaciously following through, and ensuring accountability."[35]

35 Larry Bossidy, Ram Charan, and Charles Burck, *Execution: The Discipline of Getting Things Done* (Crown Business, 2002).

TAKEAWAYS

- Find your leadership tribe. As a leader, it makes sense to make authentic connections. Build a team that wants to work with you and will support you.
- Growth thrives in discomfort, so get out of your comfort zone. Find a way to be at ease during change and transition.
- Be actively kind as you take action. Make those hard decisions, but always act from the perspective of the organization and not your own self-interest.

WHAT'S NEXT

We've just looked at how you can control your individual reactions in the necessary goodbye. Next, we'll examine how the team participates.

CHAPTER 17

THE ROLE OF THE TEAM

The main ingredient of stardom is the rest of the team. –John Wooden

"Know thyself" has been inscribed upon the Temple of Apollo in the ancient Greek precinct of Delphi since the fifth century BC. If you asked Socrates, he would tell you it means being active, rational, practical, and constructive. If you ask me, I would say it means knowing where you are great. Where you could stumble. Knowing your gifts, talents, and abilities. Knowing your place. Embracing your values and emotions. Owning that you are human. It is OK to let others know what you don't know. When you see yourself as others see you, you can better see others and their perspectives for what they are and what they have the potential to be.

There is a panoply of tools (some are free online) out there that can help you better know yourself. The Myers–Briggs Type Indicator is a famous, effective, and widely used personality test—developed in

1943 by a mother-and-daughter team to support recruitment during World War II—for leadership and employment. DISC is a profiling tool that was first proposed in 1928 and is one of the simplest out there, with only four personality types. Gallup's CliftonStrengths (formerly called StrengthsFinder) helps you find your strengths from a long list, including strategy, responsibility, positivity, and self-assurance. The True Colors Test assigns you a color to help you learn more about how you react in anticipated and unexpected situations. Are you a blue or a gold? You can dive deeper into your Jungian profile or work with Indigenous people skilled with totems. This is all about building your emotional intelligence. To help you build strong relationships. To meet your goals. To succeed in your role. And to grow your career.

No assessment works independently and provides all the answers to your inner self. Having said that, I am particularly fond of the Hogan Assessment. It is also trusted by 75 percent of the Fortune 500. It examines your personality from every angle. The personality you formed—and that was formed for you—by both nature and nurture by the age of five. The bright side. The dark side. The inside. Your identity. Your reputation. Your cognitive skills. There are three tests in the Hogan Assessment—the Hogan Personality Inventory, the Hogan Development Survey, and the Motives, Values, Preferences Inventory.[36] Drs. Robert and Joyce Hogan successfully challenged decades of dogma by showing that personality predicts job performance. Unlike IQ tests, personality assessments do so without discriminating against different groups. Ever since the tool became available in 1987, more

---

36 Robert Hogan and Joyce Hogan, "The Hogan Personality Inventory," in *Big Five Assessment*, ed. Boele de Raad and Marco Perugini (Hogrefe & Huber Publishers, 2002), 329–346.

than eleven million people worldwide have used it. You can't fool this assessment. It never lies.

Once you have yourself figured out (that's a joke … it's more like a safari than a test or assessment), all leaders need a solid professional network. Most leaders ignore this necessity. You deserve your very own cabinet. Find people whom you can count on. Reach out to them when you need a willing ear, sage advice, or a helping hand with the strategy, operations, and people issues you are facing. Use them when mulling over a decision, exploring options, or considering taking action with those nonperformers. They are your unbiased sounding board. You don't have to do whatever they say. That's the beauty of it. Free advice from people you respect. You might want to consider any and all (the more and broader the merrier) of the following when building your network:

- mentors
- outside peers
- classmates
- former bosses
- consultants
- key insiders
- connectors
- executive search firms

I have been part of an unrepeatable network thanks to the Kaiser Institute—the late Dr. Leland Kaiser, Leanne Kaiser Carlson, and Kevin Kaiser. I cocreated a community network in northwestern New Jersey in the 1990s to improve health in three counties with a member of my personal network to this day, along with the skilled facilitation of Leanne and Kevin. We have fostered high-performing teams with Leanne and Kevin by exploring issues of trust, relationships, context, tendencies, boundaries, glitches, tough rubs, collaboration versus autonomy, and totems. The network they birthed is called the Alembic Coterie. An alembic is an alchemical still. A coterie is an intimate group with a unifying common interest. This is a collection of system leaders, innovators, entrepreneurs, and unusual thinkers. We are all knee-deep in designing and transmuting in dense parts of the world. Probing the deep layers of reality. This was my tribe when I was gifted my wand. Together, we go beyond the ordinary and lead on the most intriguing edges.

COACHES

An executive coach is another valuable asset, depending on where you sit on the organizational chart. The right coach and the right coaching. There are way too many fakers out there. Ensure the coach aligns with your expertise, position, and industry. It helps when they have sat in your seat. If you are a CEO, former CEOs know what you are dealing with. Ensure they have real credentials and solid advanced training in coaching. Bill Belichick didn't just appear at the New England Patriots and start winning. He was fired by the Cleveland Browns five years before arriving in Foxborough. Peyton Manning didn't employ a college swimming coach to help him continually hone his quarterback skills. Tiger Woods had coaches for every one of his fifteen professional major golf championships and eighty-two PGA Tour wins. Why wouldn't you have a leadership coach? Interview potential coaches. Find out what assessment tools they use to kick things off and keep things going. Know how they use the tools. Dive into their thoughts on leadership and your path specifically. Finally, do you like being around the person? You will be spending tons of time up front and early in the process with this person. You will be spending even more time with them when you are debating acting on individual leader and team issues.

Recipe for Success

Only now are you ready to assemble the ingredients for John Wooden stardom—the rest of the team. My oldest son, a classically trained chef from the Culinary Institute of America (the legit CIA), tells me this is called *mise en place*, French for "putting in place or gathering." Read the entire recipe. Prepare your workspace. Prepare the equipment. Gather ingredients. Prepare the ingredients and place them neatly in bowls. Begin cooking. Clean as you go.

The featured ingredient for building your team is hiring slowly. Like really slowly. Before you even launch with HR or a search firm, the team and you need to be aligned around what you are looking for, what you need, and what type of person is best suited for the seat, depending on where the bus is headed. Do they need to have done the job before, or is someone on the way up with the right skills the way to go? How important is their alignment with the organization's mission, vision, and values? What archetype is best for this position? Are you missing a Rebel, Joker, or Creator? What are the key skill sets and experiences the person must bring on the bus? What will success look like after the first year?

If you are the hiring leader, you are responsible for the process. Not HR. Not the team. Not a committee. Hiring is your decision with input from key stakeholders. You never delegate this core leadership responsibility. Once you have the criteria, work through a process to ensure that every person in the final candidate pool is someone you can work with. Your one-on-one interviews with candidates are essential. Not just one or just one hour. You should get at least three (if not five) shots throughout the entire process of spending time with the person. For you to honestly know them. For them to truly know you as their potential new boss. Your interview is not enough. Get the whole team involved—their peers, their direct reports, and other key stakeholders (maybe even the board for COO and CFO roles). Remember that people leave bosses and teams. Don't confuse team interviews with panel interviews. They could be. They don't always have to be. It is a chance for both sides to talk about the role, observe individual and team dynamics, and gauge fit. While making the decision, the team will give you feedback on what you noticed and, more often than not, new observations that they picked up through their unique lens. It also provides job seekers with a preview of what it will be like working with their potential future colleagues.

Never Trust Your Gut in Hiring Decisions

All hiring decisions are important. There is a science to hiring people. Back to the assessments. Your HR team can make this standard practice for all hiring, or you can engage professionals (with advanced education and training) in organizational psychology to assist you in diving deeper for those more critical and senior hires. This process (no less than four hours and no more than a full workday) usually takes the form of using technology, virtual meetings, and live discussions around a variety of assessments, role-playing, case studies, and business reviews.

A customized and integrated assessment is another set of quantitative and qualitative hiring (and development) data points for you and the team. A more precise tool for your final interviews and scientific feedback for behavioral interviewing. You can more easily focus on the candidate's past experiences, how they have navigated certain situations, and how they will utilize skills relevant to the future position. Do they know their strengths? More importantly, do they know their weaknesses? What have they done to fix them or mitigate them? Are they self-aware? How would they handle the real and practical rather than the theoretical or hypothetical? Are they the right cultural fit? Have they done the job, and can they stretch in this new position? What development will they need from you and others if you ultimately choose them for the role?

Marriott International—with premium brands such as Ritz-Carlton, St. Regis, and The Luxury Collection—has honed this exact process to make an offer within eight weeks or less after the initial application. They evaluate fit for the position based on criteria and then conduct phone screenings. They put all potential candidates through a formal assessment process. If you aren't service-oriented, you are probably not the best fit for a company with $24 billion in revenue across thirty brands with almost nine thousand locations and 1.6 million rooms across its ecosystem. To get that offer, you will go through several interviews, all rooted in the STAR framework—situations (S) you have experienced, tasks (T) you have been assigned in your work life, actions (A) you have taken to manage and solve those problems, and results (R) you have achieved. Results matter, not just in leadership.

If you make it to the coveted title of CEO, there will only be two things that you truly control—what your office looks like and who serves on your team. I've worked in an organization where I controlled neither (thanks to the Creator from a previous chapter). The team (not what your office looks like) is right where DEI, welcoming, and belonging enter the thought processes. It is not a string of letters or a fad. Giving a voice to those who don't have a voice. Companies formally committed to and taking action based on DEI are 37 percent more productive, make 87 percent better decisions, and have a 39 percent increased likelihood of outperforming companies that don't uphold DEI policies at all or say they do without action. These inclusive organizations have 60 percent better performance across the entire service-profit chain (work environment, engagement, quality, customer satisfaction, loyalty, growth, and that bottom line).[37] Do you want to make better decisions? Can your organization be more productive? Do you want to increase your likelihood of success? Do you want to succeed? The team and how you construct drive (most of) that.

Instead of getting caught up in the jargon and lingo, read the 2005 book by Pulitzer Prize–winning American historian Doris Kearns Goodwin, *Team of Rivals: The Political Genius of Abraham Lincoln*. While President Lincoln's team consisted of all white men (context matters here), he brought together a group of leaders with tumultuous relationships from widely varying backgrounds, perspectives, and ideologies at a time of presidential and national complexity like we hadn't seen in our country's first century. He turned critics into allies with the understanding that collaboration and autonomy are two sides of the same leadership coin. The more collaborative you are, the more autonomous you can be. It was a room full of ambition and ego. Secretary of War Edwin Stanton hated Lincoln, his former

---

37 Ron Carucci, "One More Time: Why Diversity Leads To Better Team Performance," *Forbes*, January 24, 2024, https://www.forbes.com/sites/roncarucci/2024/01/24/one-more-time-why-diversity-leads-to-better-team-performance/.

colleague in the legal profession. But Lincoln knew that Stanton was relentless and disciplined, which provided the perfect balance to his own tolerance and moderation. From *Team of Rivals*: "As a leader, it can be tempting to have an inner circle of 'Yes' [people]. However, having people who aren't afraid to question your motives or assumptions can ultimately lead to greater outcomes as ideas are thrashed out freely."[38] High-performing teams—ones with a diverse set of people, personalities, and capabilities—take the time to understand all perspectives, collaborate, cross swords, and settle differences inside the room. They are always deeply aligned outside the room, and they execute and deliver results together.

Why Teams Fall Apart

I am sure you didn't court your spouse or significant other before the nuptials and then abandon them after the honeymoon. Or maybe you did. Today, half of all marriages end in divorce or separation—41 percent of first marriages, 60 percent of second marriages, and 73 percent of third marriages.[39] The superstition that the third time is the charm is false. Marriages fail because of a lack of preparation, unrealistic expectations, financial troubles, poor communication, inequality, constant arguing, and infidelity.

Teams fail for the exact same reasons as marriages and in the same percentages. There are very few high-performing leadership teams.

---

38 Doris Kearns Goodwin, *Team of Rivals: The Political Genius of Abraham Lincoln* (Simon & Schuster, 2005).

39 "Divorce Statistics: Over 115 Studies, Facts and Rates for 2024," Wilkinson & Finkbeiner Family Law Attorneys, accessed August 26, 2025, https://www.wf-lawyers.com/divorce-statistics-and-facts/.

You are lucky if you sit on one. But it isn't luck at all. Court your team, like you did in the hiring process and the honeymoon. Show them the love. They say that time heals all wounds. Time builds trust and loyalty within a team. The investment of time is an investment in the team's success (and your success).

According to research, 99.1 percent of people want to be part of an organization that nourishes communication. Who are the 0.9 percent? Read the previous chapters to find out. Those personality assessments will call them out. Effective organizational and team communication generates 4.5 times greater talent retention. Teamwork is the most important criterion (when choosing a job and deciding to stay with an organization) for two in five employees. More than 80 percent of today's employees view online collaboration tools positively.[40]

Spend time with your team individually. For established players, at least an hour a month. For newer members, at least an hour every two weeks. Let them drive the agenda. Get your team together as routinely. One hour a week doesn't work. It doesn't get you a team that can get into messy issues and contentious dialogue. With my senior teams, we like to spend around twelve hours a month with just us, as a team. One full day and then one-half day. We codesigned a standard agenda format. We developed guiding principles and working norms for the meetings. No phones in the meetings. No outsiders or presenters. No reports (you can read those via email). We "advance" twice a year for three days each time. One of the advances includes family. We always build in time in the afternoons for activities together. The first two days are strictly focused on the team. No issues, topics, or problems. Our development together, individually

40 "Teamwork Statistics 2024: Importance of Collaboration," TeamStage, accessed August 26, 2025, https://teamstage.io/teamwork-statistics/.

and collectively. The third day is time for dialogue with an outside expert about industry trends, radical thinking, strategic thinking, financial imperatives, or the latest acquisition target.

Build the Team, and the Team Will Do the Cooking

Mise en place. There is a high level of trust, collaboration, welcoming, and belonging. They take responsibility for their work and the work of the team. Hold each other accountable. Ensure continuous improvement. High-performing teams are exceptional at identifying and solving problems. When results aren't happening, or an individual isn't holding up their end of the commitment, they will let you know. Efficient and effective teams are far less forgiving than bosses. This is where you play President Lincoln, who paid no attention to personal differences or past slights. He loathed holding a grudge. You are the coach and executive chef (not the supervisor or, worse yet, stupid-visor). Thinking (heads up), focus, kindness, relationships, and alignment are the soft skills to bring to the team. Your action to-do list is communication, trust, and accountability.

If you are doing the right things, the team will gladly help you clean as you go. I abhor doing dishes. It is a chore. Tedious. It can take hours, especially on holidays. Painful. It is not something I do sometimes. Never. When my parents married in the 1960s, my father promised my mother an electric dishwasher if he didn't have to do the dishes. The apple never falls far from the tree. There should be a circle of Hell for people like me. With all difficult decisions, especially deselecting a key team member, the team will be right there with you every step of the way with the cleanup. Always engage and use the team. Early and often, such as voting in certain city and state politics. HR and legal will be at your side. The communications team will craft the right messaging. The team will help you navigate all the stakeholders. They will know the departing individual and what matters most to them (because they are already talking to them and they are talking to the team). They will see things you will miss. *Mise en place.*

TAKEAWAYS

- Use available personality assessment tools to understand yourself and your team.
- Take the effort to be part of a solid professional network.
- Invest in an experienced HR team that uses methods based on organizational psychology to create effective hiring processes.

WHAT'S NEXT

We've looked at the best ways, as a leader, to use your team. Now, we will look at the resistance you will encounter from all sides.

CHAPTER 18

RESISTANCE IS FUTILE

There's sharks and minnows in this world ... and if you don't know which one you are, then you ain't a shark. –**Rip Wheeler, Yellowstone**

In *Star Trek: The Next Generation*, a recurring antagonist is the Borg, who commonly say, "Resistance is futile!" In the singular pursuit of perfection at all costs, the Borg co-opt technology and other species through assimilation. They inject nanoprobes into victims' bodies and surgically augment them with cybernetic components. The Borg make the Klingons and Romulans look like Little Leaguers.

The Borg clearly understood Newton's third law of motion. The law of action and reaction was first presented in *Principia Mathematica Philosophiae Naturalis* in 1686. For every action, there is an equal and opposite reaction. FA = –FB. If Person A exerts a force on Person B, then Person B also exerts an equal and opposite (i.e., negative) force on Person A.

Newton's third law explains many sports injuries. Every time your feet hit the ground while running, the ground hits your feet with an equal and opposite force. When you swing your pickleball paddle, your arm receives the same force in return. That's why orthopedists are always busy and do well financially. When your car is rear-ended, the moving vehicle exerts a tremendous force on the stationary car. The stationary car exerts an equal and opposite force on the moving vehicle. Both cars are damaged in the process.

Think about someone pushing on you. It may be literally when you are on a crowded subway. It could be figuratively being pressed with a deadline and a tight budget on a high-profile project. What happens to your body? You respond with an equal and opposite force. Fight or flight. You go on high alert. DEFCON 1 and immediate readiness for war. Your brain releases signals to your body. You start breathing heavily and rapidly. Your heart rate and blood pressure go up. Your muscles become tense and rigid. You may turn pale or flushed. The more they push, the more you are ready to act in retaliation. This is exhausting, decreases your resilience, and burns you out. Being pushed—literally or figuratively—is depressing.

Rumors, Detractors, and Nemeses

Those who don't want your tough decisions and much-needed changes don't understand *Star Trek*, let alone the fundamental laws of physics. The gossipers will slither out from under the rocks. Seizing power by having the latest scoop. Using this info to initiate unfounded rumors. The rumormongers will emerge from the woodwork. Keeping the rumors going even when they are false. Laying their foundation in the name of their truth and aimed at damaging you.

Back-channelers, those who are not in the actual sphere of influence but are threatened or slighted, will be animated. Taking more extensive discussions into secret (with some grains of truth sprinkled in) and spurring conflict.

This is also a well-timed opening for your detractors to get an audience. Expressing this discontent with you, the decision, and past transgressions openly and negatively. Encouraging others to disengage and maybe getting some traction. Your nemeses, those rivals who always seem to be able to get the best of you (not to be confused with enemies), will seize the opportunity to heighten competition with you, fluster you, and finish ahead of you. Your enemies have been poised for an opening and will use the situation, depending on how charged it is, to take you down. Doing almost anything, including the unethical, immoral, and just plain unkind, to seize your power and control.

Listen carefully. Know the meetings after the meeting. Talk to anyone and everyone. This is the time to use your well-cultivated network and expand it. Shore up your relationships. Ask lots of questions. Be sure you know what is being said about you. Take the grains of truth in the rumors and gossip. Line up your "votes," especially with powerful people, both formal and informal. Sun Tzu, a Chinese general, strategist, and philosopher who is believed to be the author of *The Art of War,* written between 475 and 221 BC, is credited with the phrase, "Keep your friends close; keep your enemies closer." Keep your actual and suspected traitors closer—the non-loyal, uncommitted, secretive, suspicious, dishonest, deceitful, chronically negative, and regularly undermining. But tread cautiously. Watch your front, back, and sides. Be hyper-political.

At some point, you will find yourself uttering the words of David Rose (played by Dan Levy) in *Schitt's Creek*: "I'm starting to feel like I'm trapped in an Avril Lavigne lyric here." You are trapped. Resistance is complicated. Lavigne's debut single from her debut album in 2002 asks the right questions. To paraphrase, it is all about asking why you are surrounded by fake people who complicate things to a frustrating level. If you guessed the lyrics based on that cryptic clue, full marks to you!

Sun Tzu revolutionized the complications of war and combat. There are no records in Chinese history of him and his army ever losing a battle. Many elements from his strategy—planning and resource management in particular—are used today in global security issues, regional conflicts, attempts to make our world safer and more peaceful, and in diverse nonmilitary settings. Sun Tzu says the following about resistance:[41]

- Know thyself, know thy enemy. A thousand battles, a thousand victories.
- If you know yourself but not the enemy, for every victory gained, you will also suffer a defeat.
- If you know neither the enemy nor yourself, you will succumb in every battle.
- Victorious warriors win first and then go to war, while defeated warriors go to war first and then seek to win.
- To win one hundred victories in one hundred battles is not the acme of skill. To subdue the enemy without fighting is the acme of skill.

41 Gerald A. Michaelson and Steven W. Michaelson, *Sun Tzu—The Art of War for Managers: 50 Strategic Rules* (Adams Media, 2010).

- Be extremely subtle, even to the point of formlessness. Be extremely mysterious, even to the point of soundlessness. Thereby, you can be the director of the opponent's fate.
- The supreme art of war is to subdue the enemy without fighting.

Be the Shark

Lean into the resistance. Run toward it. Our national tendency is to withdraw and run away when anything gets difficult. That disconnects us from all the right people and requisite resources that we need the most in the mess. Also, stay connected to the gossipers, rumormongers, nemeses, enemies, and traitors. Get a closer view. Be subtle and mysterious. Own what you are doing (and who you eliminate from the team) with love and a sense of unification. Enjoy being the center of the action when the time is right. Work densely and strongly. Win first and then go to war. Subdue your resistance without fighting.

You are the shark, not a minnow. While the shark can be a skilled solitary hunter, it forms a group to play defense and offense. Play in deeper water. You are the better swimmer and have far more at your disposal. You have all the information that those working against you do not have. They are working based on limited facts. Activate leadership camouflage to give yourself agility, adaptability, and speed. Wait from below and behind. Stealth and surprise are your gifts. Bump those resisting the change to let them know you are there. Bumping compels you to be highly curious, detailed, and cognitive. Thoughtful, deliberate, and doggedly factual. When the decision is executed, move to the center to take on your prey. Swim short distances. Bite hard with confidence. Your patient, yet adept, Sun Tzu bumping may injure them, cause them to retreat, and even foil their plans without the need to show your teeth at all.

TAKEAWAYS

- Understand that there will always be detractors.
- Lean into the resistance. Never turn your back on it.
- Be a shark and not a minnow. Own your decisions. Assert yourself. Once your organizational strategies start picking up speed and succeeding, you will have won the war without an overt fight.

WHAT'S NEXT

The problem team member is not going anywhere on their own. Here's how you can start the process in a kind but effective way.

CHAPTER 19

THE BLIND EYE

Weak people revenge. Strong people forgive. Intelligent people ignore. –Albert Einstein

Hit the pause button now on the call to action and bite hard. There is a cold, hard leadership truth here. You can't always take action, especially when promptly addressing people's issues. We have to play politics too. Organizational politics aren't inherently evil. No need to give up your throne and be the self-sabotaging Ruler.

The Rule of Three

Priorities matter. Leaders are responsible for focusing the team and, at the same time, removing barriers and lessening distractions. The rule of three is a writing principle rooted in the concept that we all process information by recognizing patterns. Three is the smallest number where we can recognize a pattern. The rule of three, in psychology, asserts that ideas given in threes are more memorable and exciting. I once attended a church where a friar embraced this in his sermons. It worked. I stayed awake and remembered them for at least seventy-two hours. The rule of three works in prioritization at home (with the to-do list) and at work (with how you focus). You might as well have no priorities when you have a laundry list of a hundred priorities. The likelihood of you processing more than three priorities and being interested in (let alone accomplishing them) is zero.

In his immortal 1970 essay on servant leadership, Robert K. Greenleaf narrowed it down from three to only one: "The ability to withdraw and reorient oneself, if only for a moment, presumes that one has learned 'The Art of Systematic Neglect,' to sort out the more important from the less important—and the important from the urgent—and attend to the more important, even though there may be penalties and censure for the neglect of something else."[42] The reality is that replacing the nonperforming leader may be barely important and unambiguously not urgent. You can justifiably avoid declining their contract extension decision by spending your valuable and limited time on more important and urgent matters. The one or the top three. Be aware that there are penalties and criticism for neglecting the individual and the team over other priorities.

Political Capital

What's in your wallet? In *Political Influence* from 1961, Edward C. Banfield (best known for *The Moral Basis of a Backward Society* and *The*

42 Greenleaf, *Servant Leadership.*

Unheavenly City) first introduced the concept of political capital. In political theory, political capital is "a stock of influence" built here and there from the many and others who were endowed by position, title, or circumstance. It can be used for exchanges between politicians and between politicians and constituents. However, it's been around since the first tribe came together. Influencing the group to go to war with a neighboring tribe (quite possibly for no good reason other than ego and power) is tribal political power. Like it or not, political capital is one of the currencies of modern office life. You accumulate resources and power through relationships, trust, goodwill, and influence.

When you are in a new role, your political capital account starts at full. You use this currency when making decisions, aligning the team, achieving changes, and forging your new leadership direction. Think of it as credit. You can bank it, save it, invest it, spend it, misspend it, and lose it. When dancing around a people decision, you may not want to use your political capital at that moment. Some people changes will cost more than others. You don't want to use up most or all of your capital on one or two people. Maybe you can't afford a mistake (or another mistake). You may have used too much of your political capital to afford the next move.

While this is the urgent priority for you (and even your whole team) and you are willing and able to use your political capital, 86ing still may not be in the cards. I know they are consistently doing abysmal work, and their attitude is atrocious. Take a deep breath. In these cases, the person has more power (and influence) than you. With those above you, including the board, CEO, more senior executives, donors, shareholders, or big shots in the community. This still very much happens today, more than we would like to think. Some people in organizations are protected and guarded by very important people (VIPs). One of the deplorable leaders featured in one of the archetypes was a relative of one of the organization's founders. I've seen people married to relatives of VIPs. They may vacation, play golf, or go duck hunting with VIPs. Their kids may go to the same school. They may attend the same church. They were sorority sisters in college. Their spouses or significant others are besties. It doesn't matter what it is. It is what it is. Don't ever jeopardize yourself and the organization over the politics of retrenching someone.

What Not to Do

This doesn't mean you are off the hook and can avoid taking action. There are first-rate (not all kind or nice) strategies to solve your problem while not "borrowing trouble" (a good Southern proverb). Before we discuss what to do, please never do any of the following:

1. Do not transfer them to another team inside the organization. Great companies don't transfer problem employees. Lazy leaders do. Passing the buck isn't the solution. Don't make your problem someone else's problem. It will still be your problem.

2. Do not mess with their pay. While reducing someone's pay can be done legally, this is imbecilic leadership. And it just isn't kind. Forget about the trust continuum. You just killed your credibility and reputation entirely with a pay cut. Forget goals or results. Forget having productive conversations. Talk about getting a bad attitude in return. The famous words from Judge Elihu Smails (the eternally funny Ted Knight) to his nephew, Spaulding, in the 1980 movie *Caddyshack*, ring true: "You will get nothing and like it!"

3. Do not mess with their title. While you should never meddle with people's money, playing around with their title is not kind either. Titles are important to many people. They give them meaning and a perception of value by themselves and others. They make them feel important at work. Be nice here.

Diminish Their Responsibilities

Narrow their scope of responsibility. Diminish their direct reporting relationships. Set tight boundaries to keep things (their impact on others) in and, in turn, keep things (their performance and behavior) out. Get them into a clear and defined box. Inside the box, keep it limited to things that don't matter. Or, better yet, the minor things so that, if they fail, it is not a disaster. My father, an elementary school teacher, called this "busywork." He felt that lazy teachers assigned busywork to students. You can't let this individual even remotely close to vital organizational priorities. Even more so, you have to keep them out of the things that you are personally working on. This is lazy leadership, too, but effective for you and the team.

Further Isolate Them

If tightening up their core responsibilities isn't yielding the intended results, take them out of projects, meetings, and discussions. Keep them on the periphery and away from the circle of action. You don't want them to be necessary. They weren't reliable and did not deliver results in the first place. You also don't want them to be relevant. Disconnect them from the pressing people and situations. This doesn't smell like *kind.* Isolating them smells like abuse—emotional, physical, control, jealousy, manipulation, and gaslighting. There is a fine line here. This isn't about you and them. This is about the organization and the team. Do your best to do this with kindness. At a minimum, nicely.

Offer Unvarnished Feedback

Proffer direct and (painfully) blunt observations. Not yours alone. Use 360-degree feedback from their team. Your HR team may have a solid process, but a third party with tools (and training in business psychology) is far more helpful in these sticky predicaments. Quantitative feedback in survey form. Have the facilitator use quantitative feedback to interview people to build out the survey findings more robustly. For both the survey and interviews, let them pick the participants. Just be sure to get feedback from them, their peers, their direct reports, their customers, and yourself. A complete picture. This is not about what you think. You need to provide them with a clear reflection on how they are performing (from all potential perspectives). Get it out there, in a data-informed way, how they are being perceived and how their self-perceptions align with those of others.

Repeat Yourself ... Often

Be clear about your expectations and boundaries. You are going to have to repeat yourself several times. No rule of three here. The rule of seven. In marketing, customers should encounter a brand's message at least seven times before they can make a decision. And even that won't always work. When people aren't performing, most of them know it. To avoid the conversation, they will change the terms, run their agenda, avoid the real issues, and do all of it in conflict-avoidant, passive-aggressive, and behind-the-scenes ways. Hold your ground, dig in deep, and prepare yourself to say "no" more than feels comfortable. Have a plan for when the conversations and interactions aren't going well, and your repetitive boundary setting isn't holding firm.

Change Their Reporting Relationship

Rarely do people who have been diminished, isolated, confronted with frank feedback, and treated with sharp elbows leave the organization on their own. The higher up, the bigger the title, the more the pay, and the bigger the ego … the more absolute that statement becomes. You are stuck. You have done everything you can, but the team can't cook something up or clean up the mess. This connected troublemaker impacts you, your work, your emotional health, your mental health, and your personal life.

We talked through this already—it is never OK to transfer the person. Transferring their reporting relationship to someone else on your team, on the other hand, is OK. Maybe you aren't the right person to manage them in the first place. Your wrath isn't helpful anymore. Maybe the next supervisor will be more successful in keeping them from getting in the way. Perhaps the other person will find a healthier relationship and make the turn (even a little turn).

If the organization has put handcuffs on you around one person, you have to do what it takes to make it work for the rest of the team and your own sanity. Just always be true to yourself. Keep talking the talk and walking the walk. Use words and actions even when it feels a bit dirty or like it is dipping into unkind territory. People need to know where you stand in this tight spot. It allows them to get more realistic about you and your expectations. Emotions can't get the best of you. Sarcasm never passes off as a sense of humor. Cop to the charge that the quandary is yours. All yours. You aren't admitting you are wrong and that others are right. You are admitting the situation exists. No need to make this personal and settle scores. This isn't a win or lose matter. Don't hold grudges. Your goal should be to let the small and big stuff go to help everyone win as best as you and they can. Stay humble and grounded. Build your reputation and brand as a trusted leader. Laugh at yourself along the way.

TAKEAWAYS

- Use your political capital wisely.
- Do not jeopardize your career or the company over the politics of retrenching someone.
- If you cannot fire them, change who they report to.

WHAT'S NEXT

It's time to do it. Here's a guide, step-by-step.

CHAPTER 20

GETTING IT RIGHT

I follow three rules—do the right thing, do the best you can, and always show people you care. —Lou Holtz

According to Mercer, a health benefits, investments, retirement, M&A, and workforce and careers advisory services firm, people voluntarily leave leadership at 3.6 times the rate that we deliver on the involuntary option (17.3 percent voluntary turnover versus 4.8 percent involuntary turnover in 2023).[43]

There is extensive research on executive failure rates by the Center for Creative Leadership (which can directly trace its roots to Vicks VapoRub in 1894), which indicates failure rates ranging from 30 percent to 50 percent within the first eighteen months of

43 "How Much Turnover Is Too Much?" Mercer, September 2025, https://www.imercer.com/articleinsights/workforce-turnover-trends.

tenure.[44] Leadership IQ (founded by Mark Murphy, a *New York Times* bestselling author in leadership and engagement) conducted studies showing failure rates of 46 percent in the same period.[45] Some would argue that two-thirds of these executive failures (yes, they got fired) revolve around the lack of self-awareness and emotional intelligence, which impacts their ability to build a functioning team.

My executive coach, with whom I have worked on and off for almost two decades, constantly challenges me: "Do you want to get it right or be right?" Henry James, a fellow stream-of-consciousness writer, described a spirited young woman, Isabel Archer, in *The Portrait of a Lady* (first published as a serial in *The Atlantic Monthly* and *Macmillan's Magazine* in 1880), saying, "She had … a general idea that people were right when they treated her as if she were rather superior. Whether or not she were superior, people were right in admiring her if they thought her so … It may be affirmed without delay that Isabel was probably very liable to the sin of self-esteem; she often surveyed with complacency the field of her own nature; she was in the habit of taking for granted, on scanty evidence, that she was right; impulsively, she often admired herself."[46]

I worked with an executive who worked exclusively in the "being right" place. We didn't even remotely get along, and it was obvious to both of us. Some people just need to be right. Too many leaders always want to be right. Having all the answers all the time. No creativity

---

44 Melanie Hughes, "How Executives Can Measure Success in the First Six Months," *Forbes*, January 2024, https://www.forbes.com/sites/melaniehughes/2024/01/18/how-executives-can-measure-success-in-the-first-6-months/.

45 "Leadership IQ Study: Why New Hires Fail," WorkComp Professionals, May 2010, https://www.workcompprofessionals.com/advisory/archive-0000/L5eBull2010/May/2010_05_a5.html.

46 Henry James, *The Portrait of a Lady* (Houghton, Mifflin and Company, 1881).

is needed. No questions need to be asked by the team. Who needs feedback … ever? Sparse evidence when making your decisions or, more often than not, your proclamations. This is how it is. This is how it is going to be. Filled with ego (it filled the building and beyond) and an authoritarian righteousness. This executive once asked me, a peer in another organization, why I did not like them, because, apparently, everyone else liked them. Trust me, they were the direct opposite of a people pleaser. I didn't have the heart to tell them that most people didn't like them too. I don't believe even their spouse and their children liked them. When you are dealing with someone who always has to be right, you are forced to make them right (especially if you want to keep your job). When you always have to be right, resistance and conflict are attracted to you. Cooperation, commitment, trust, and opinions other than your own are repelled by you. They were a smart, capable, gifted, and surprisingly successful executive. It was depressing to see them gradually disconnect themselves from everyone and everything that could have boosted their success.

Remove Your Ego from the Outcome

Don't be right. Get it right. Remove ego from the outcome. It is not about you. It is never about you as a leader. Ask lots of questions. Preferably open-ended questions; yes/no questions limit possibilities. When asked a question, be affirmative (that means a "yes") and keep the conversation open (that means following "yes" with an "and"). Create a safe environment in which information and feedback flow freely (even if what you hear or see hurts). Create an environment in which others and your team get to the correct answer.

Asking Someone to Leave

Get it right when asking someone to leave the organization. There is never a right time to do the wrong thing. There is never a wrong time to do the right thing. Life presents us with countless difficult decisions. Dumping someone is right there at the top. When grappling with the best path, concentrate on doing what's right (and aligning the decisions with yours and the organization's values and ethics). Do it the best way possible. You aren't going to be perfect, but don't let that (or anyone or anything) stop you from giving it everything you have. Do it in a way that shows the individual and team that you genuinely care. Mean what you say. Take the time to listen to their concerns and offer your support where needed.

There is a superfluity of books by HR professionals, lawyers, consultants, and motivational speakers on how to get it right. They are all helpful, but they are just not sufficient. Unless you have done this yourself (and done it many times) and had it done to you, you are missing something. Here is the bigger and more complete picture.

Take Your Temperature

You need to ask yourself the gritty questions and tell yourself the cold, hard truth. How do you feel about the situation, and what do you need to do? Are you uncomfortable? That's good. Keep going. Did you give it your all with this individual? How long did you try to make this work? Do you or they need more time? Do you have any biases that are creeping into this decision? Is there anything you need to forgive yourself for? What do you need to do to take care of yourself and manage this complicated matter? What do you need to let go of in the process and afterward? What are you grateful for?

Take the Team's Temperature

Use similar questions to ask your team how they feel about the situation and the decisions that need to be made. Confidentiality is important. You painting a more complete picture with your team is absolutely critical. How do they feel about the problem? What thoughts do they have on the solutions? What are they hearing from the impacted individual? And key stakeholders? Who is already on board? Who needs more time and more discussion? Are they comfortable or uncomfortable, or even comfortable with being uncomfortable? What would get them comfortable? Where is the resistance? What won't be helpful to the team? How do you need to stay connected to the team during the process? What communication is required?

HR and Legal

You need HR, legal, corporate compliance, and communications from the beginning. Also, consider the role the board and other leaders (above you, below you, and your peers) need to play in your process. It never hurts to check in with them to hear whether they have your back, think it might be a bad idea, or believe they don't need to be involved at all. What other functional groups are impacted by your decision? HR, legal, etc., are powerful, specialized professionals dedicated to helping you shape the process by building and ensuring the clarity of the conversation. They mitigate, minimize, and eliminate potential damage to the employee, the company, and you. However, they don't make the decision (their input is valuable), and following through is not their responsibility. They aren't there to make the task more pleasant for you or anyone else involved.

Be Kind

How can you best be kind to the individual impacted? How can you be kind to your team? How can you be kinder to yourself in the process? Self-kindness never hurts. Kindness is contagious. Kindness is necessary for the person leaving the organization. Kindness means not making this decision and your conversation a surprise. When it comes to this, it should be clear that this is about performance, fit, the business, the future of the team, and/or even circumstances beyond their control. Be prepared to have answers available to all their potential questions at the meeting (delivered by HR). Be fair and respectful. Allow the impacted individual the time and space to process (just not in the discussion meeting itself). Offer your support and the support of the organization in their transition. Brené Brown, author of *Dare to Lead*, said it best: "A deep sense of love and belonging is an irreducible need of all people. We are biologically, cognitively, physically, and spiritually wired to love, to be loved, and to belong. When those needs are not met, we don't function as we were meant to. We break. We fall apart. We numb. We ache. We hurt others. We get sick."[47] Being fired is a uniquely numbing experience. Be kind to change that. Clear is kind. Unclear is unkind.

---

47 Brené Brown, *Dare to Lead* (Vermilion, 2018).

Time for Patience

This is the point where you pause to reflect and discern. You can do it yourself. You can do it with the team working with you on this. You can do it with your external network. Preferably, all of the above. The wider your circle—understanding the immensely confidential nature of this subject—the better off you are and the smoother the entire process. What is the central question here? How does this individual impact the organization, team, and others? Which stakeholders have been involved so far? Which other stakeholders might you have missed and need to connect with (sooner rather than later)? Have you considered all the facts? What are the values, ethics, morals, etc., at play here? Are you aligned with those organizationally? Are you aligned with what you stand for personally and as a leader? What are all the options and alternatives? Should you provide more coaching and nurturing, take a political approach and isolate the leader, or is now the time to pull the plug? What are the specific decisions you are making, and more importantly ... why? Be specific about the "why." What's your communication plan with the individual and all the key stakeholders? Do all the homework. Consider all the ways this may go. Leave nothing to chance. Use this patient reflection and discernment process to put together a detailed plan (preferably in writing, including responsibilities and timelines) on how to make it happen. Hopefully, you live to tell the story.

Points of Resistance

Dr. William Bridges, a proven authority on leading change in work and life (his 1980 book *Transitions: Making Sense of Life's Changes* sits right underneath *Compassion* on my desk), reminds us that: "Change comes more from managing the journey than from announcing the destination."[48] It is rare in your leadership journey that you won't have at least one person or a small group resist your changes. Resistance comes from fear and lack of trust. Bad timing, worries about failure, or past bad experiences. No control over, input into, consultation about, or involvement in the process and decisions. It can, directly and indirectly, be about the organizational culture and ... read this twice ... *your leadership*. They just may be close to the person leaving the organization. Listen to Green Day's "Know Your Enemy," a protest song from 2009, for the signs of resistance—model behavior, energy, silence, blindness, urgency, control, insurgency, revolt, fury, violence, and even the demons of the soul. Where could your resistance come from? What are they resisting? Why are they resisting it? Will they criticize or escalate to undermining? Will they try to reverse the decision? Will they attempt to get rid of you too? Who do you need to talk to now? And when things are happening? How can you best guide the narrative and messaging? How will you best and most politically respond if it gets bad? Do you know the enemy? Do you know your enemy?

Get Your Hands Dirty

If the person reports directly to you, be in the room (with HR and maybe even legal). While terminations should never be a surprise, be prepared for them to be surprised and for them to offer surprises of their own. Take them to your office, not some conference room or a

---

48 William Bridges, *Transitions: Making Sense of Life's Changes* (Hachette Books, 1980).

room in HR. Keep it short—around twenty minutes (preferably less). Your objective is to deliver the message and remove the employee quickly and efficiently. Remove them with kindness. Keep it sweet without sugarcoating it. No small talk. Look them in the eye. Get right to letting the individual know that they are being let go. Your tone and tempo should be clean and professional. If it is for cause (which is rare in unassigning leaders), briefly cover the violation or infractions with facts (without emotion).

If it is without cause or at will (most often the situation), there is no need to ever get into specific reasons. This is strictly a business decision. Don't defer or deflect. Don't waffle in the meeting on the decision. Don't backpedal. Don't try to soften the blow by being nice or offering "nice" concessions. Avoid a delayed departure at all costs. Nothing is ever confidential, and these delays are always clunky. It was your decision. Don't lay anything on the board, your boss, HR, or legal. This is not a crying session or an opportunity for them (or, worse yet, you) to unload insult, injury, and outrage. The impacted individual will likely have questions. If you feel the need to answer, keep it short and only to one or two questions. No lengthy discussions for you. Leave the rest for HR. You have done your part in the meeting and should step out at this point. HR (and) legal should bring with them the appropriate paperwork, information, answers, and timelines—termination letter, severance information, health insurance (COBRA) information, the process to collect company property, etc.

Times when someone other than you should be in the room to have the conversation with someone who reports directly to you are few and far between. Keep your hands clean. When Pontius Pilate (the fifth governor of the Roman province of Judaea, serving under Emperor Tiberius) saw that he was getting nowhere at the sentencing of Jesus Christ and that a riot was imminent, he took a basin of water and washed his hands in full sight of the crowd.

I am not talking about someone else (such as a peer) firing someone for you (even if you may be out of town). That was my bizarre experience. One of my Caregiver examples (who worked in HR) thought it was clever to "prefire" someone (i.e., their close friend and clique member) reporting to me before I did it. It would have been helpful to know before I met the person to terminate them. Talk about an unearthly conversation.

You definitely should wash your hands of a downscaling and let HR manage the termination process when the relationship between you and the employee being terminated is so contentious that you being in the room would only blow things up. There may be other circumstances where HR and legal advise you to avoid a riot. Don't make this the norm.

Be Kind ... Again

Always take care of the departing individual. Everyone (especially your team) watches how someone leaves the organization, even more so than how someone enters. How you do it, what you do with it, and what you say. Be fair with the severance agreement language. All too many of these important agreements are aggressively and punishingly restrictive. All too many companies vigorously and nastily negotiate the deal when the employee pushes back. Protect the company and yourself. Outcome always outweighs ego. You don't want someone losing their house, car, family, and self-esteem because of your decision. Be generous. You may need to give more than the law, policy, or agreement dictates. It isn't worth scrimping on or being frugal with other components of the departure. Continuation of health insurance. Outplacement assistance to find the next job, as well as an employee assistance program for mental and emotional support. Offer to be a reference for the individual or assist them by opening up your network to them (if the situation warrants and you feel comfortable). It's a microscopic world.

Please never pack up someone's office for them and hand them their personal items in a box during the meeting. Not kind. That is their stuff. Higher-up executives with broad power and influence should be allowed to clean out their offices over the weekend, out of sight and with dignity. Absolutely avoid walking someone out of the building (let alone having security walk them out). It's not a good look for you. It's not a healthy look for the organization.

There are times when you should not be generous during terminations. Go back to the Lover chapter for great examples. This conduct falls into abuse, abandonment, neglect, or any acts that are universally deplorable, flagrant, or outrageous by usual standards. Conduct that poses a serious risk and is hard for other colleagues to tolerate. Stealing or theft from the company. Violence or threats of violence. Providing knowingly false or misleading information. Disclosing confidential, proprietary, and/or privileged information to others (including competitors). Discrimination. Sexual and other forms of harassment. Grievous retaliation. Working under the influence of alcohol or drugs (there is a fine line here for your legal counsel), where conduct poses a serious threat to people, property, and resources. Threatening the safety and welfare of the team and the company. Felony convictions during employment. Intentionally using a position for personal gain or in a manner that damages the company's reputation (or impacts the business and operations). Send a strong message while being fiercely kind.

Honor the Room

I wish we could be excruciatingly honest when axing someone. Something comparable to the fate of William Wallace (depicted by Mel Gibson) in *Braveheart*. King Edward I of England declared him guilty of treason and sentenced him to death. Wallace was killed publicly using one of the most brutal punishments in the medieval era—hanged, drawn, and quartered. The king's communication strategy was simple—tar Wallace's head, place it on a pike on London Bridge, cut up his body, and distribute the parts to all corners of the empire. Instead, you get the privilege of personally communicating with key stakeholders (individually and in groups) and communicating in writing to broader audiences about ending the trial period.

The higher up the leader, the more the person leaving wants to write their organizational obituary. No; you write it with your communication team. Honor the room. Tell others that you know who the person was, that you respected them for who they are, and that you were grateful for what they contributed to the organization (and wish them luck in their next endeavors). Explain how the decision aligns with the organization's goals, values, and vision. Lay out the process you will use to fill the role and why (or not fill it or restructure it). Focus on the future of the team and organization, and how you will support the team, as well as how team members will support one another during the transition and beyond. Use clear, concise, and compelling language—stylistically aligned with the organization's brand and your leadership brand. Write it knowing that it will be leaked to people whom you don't want to see the communication. I always write these communications as if they will be printed on the front page of the most widely read newspaper. Avoid jargon and the temptation for ambiguity (just not King Edward I's sense of clarity).

A bonus recommendation for you and your organization on how to manage communicating downsizing. A study published in the *Strategic Management Journal* found that employees tend to distort or sugarcoat bad news because they're afraid of being viewed negatively.[49] There are no secrets in organizations. When companies dodge "honoring the room" with these huge decisions impacting lots of people, it damages the company, its reputation, and its relationships. In the absence of information from the company, people make stuff up. Avoid secrets, misinformation, and disinformation. Deliver the hard news clearly and kindly. Last I checked, everyone working in corporate America is an adult. They take it. They manage bad things in their lives. Follow the "honor the room" guidelines with your internal announcement and external press release. Once you get those out, immediately start holding regular company meetings to update employees on the implementation of layoffs and address any of their concerns. Cascade the message and ensure all leaders hold regular individual and team meetings with remaining employees to discuss any changes in roles or responsibilities and continuously reassure them about the company's future.

OK, you did it. It was grueling and a necessary burden. You mastered the least-used leadership tool. I am proud of you.

---

49 Christina Fang, Ji-Hyun (Jason) Kim, and Frances J. Milliken, "When Bad News Is Sugarcoated: Information Distortion, Organizational Search and the Behavioral Theory of the Firm," *Strategic Management Journal* 35, no. 8 (2014): 1186-1201, https://doi.org/10.1002/smj.2146.

REVIEW YOURSELF

You got it right.

You took a holistic approach to understanding relationships, patterns, and systems consistent with the teaching of Peter Senge and his *The Fifth Discipline: The Art and Practice of the Learning Organization*:[50]

- "The most effective people are those who can 'hold' their vision while remaining committed to seeing current reality."
  You understood the problem, explored all the alternatives, and remained committed.
- "Reality is made up of circles, but we see straight lines."
  You saw the situation as a whole bunch of circles and their intersections and divergences.
- "Courage is simply doing whatever is needed to pursue the vision."
  Nothing more needs to be said here. You took action and delivered the outcome.

You stayed true to yourself.

According to Carl Jung, most things are not chance or random. There is a deeper order to the universe, and its connections can't be explained by cause and effect. Call it synchronicity. OK, no more Jung.

Let's go with Joseph Jaworski's *Synchronicity: The Inner*

50 Peter Senge, *The Fifth Discipline: The Art and Practice of the Learning Organization* (Doubleday/Currency, 1990).

Path of Leadership here: "When you see what you're here for, the world begins to mirror your purpose in a magical way. It's almost as if you suddenly find yourself on a stage in a play that was written expressly for you."[51]

Practice makes permanent.
Practice does not make perfect. My father would remind us growing up that practice makes permanent. Perhaps better said in the writings of Tom Morris in *If Aristotle Ran General Motors*: "There is nothing noble in being superior to some other man. The true nobility is in being superior to your previous self."[52]

Let it go.
You patiently took the time to understand why the behaviors of others (to this point, at this point, and moving forward) make total sense. Always. All humans do things that make sense at that moment from their own frames of reference, even your detractors and mortal enemies, and especially the person being fired. You took the jabs without bruising. You worked past the resistance. You let it all go.

Sometimes, the hardest decisions we make as leaders aren't about spreadsheets or strategy. They're about people. And sometimes, the

---

51 Joseph Jaworski, *Synchronicity: The Inner Path of Leadership* (Berrett-Koehler Publishers, 2011).

52 Tom Morris, *If Aristotle Ran General Motors: The New Soul of Business* (Henry Holt and Company, 1997).

most compassionate thing we can do for someone, for our team, and for our organization is to help someone find their next chapter elsewhere. This isn't about winning or losing, heroes or villains. It's about recognizing that not every talented person belongs in every seat, and not every cultural mismatch is a character flaw. The person you're letting go isn't your enemy. They're simply someone whose story makes perfect sense from their perspective, even if it no longer aligns with yours. Let it go, not with indifference, but with the profound understanding that sometimes the best action is to give someone the freedom to find where they truly belong.

AFTERWORD

GOOD BIRTH AND GOOD DEATH

I am prepared to meet my Maker. Whether my Maker is prepared for the great ordeal of meeting me is another matter. –Winston Churchill

Entering a new relationship is an exciting, intense, and challenging experience. There is science behind this new relationship energy. Our brains are flooded with neurotransmitters and hormones—dopamine and oxytocin—giving us feelings of pleasure and relaxation. At the same time, we get spikes in cortisol and decreases in serotonin, which is much less pleasant and produces elevated anxiety and obsession. That chemical rollercoaster of new relationships is a thrill. On top of the world with the wind rushing through our hair (figuratively and occasionally literally). Blood pumping through our veins. Screams of excitement, exhilaration, and fear, fighting off losing our cookies, as we ride the highs and lows.

It is only natural for us to celebrate and applaud the "good births" in our lives. It is the human experience. The age-old baby shower is for everyone remotely close to you to "shower" you and your forthcoming child with love, blessings, games, and gifts. The whole outfitting of the new nursery is an event unto itself. What are the right crib, high chair, playpen, and stroller? You have to paint the room. What are the suitable wallpaper and carpet? Matching toys? What diaper and food brand are you going to commit to? Hook up the baby monitor and test it out. We have even invented baby reveals and gender reveals and will go to great lengths to create something new to make a splash with our family, friends, and social media. There are "babymoons" where you get away and rest before a lifetime of no sleep and anxiety. Let's not get into the extravaganza of engagements and weddings. A close colleague ensured his daughter had a personalized drone show at the wedding reception.

We put the same good birth mojo into attracting and welcoming new talent. The courting process includes several meetings, starting online and working up to in-person meetings with the entire family ... oops, team. They may only see people on "holidays," but we must introduce them. In-person interviews may include catered lunches and group dinners with appetizers, wine, expensive entrees, and desserts. We land on the candidate and then work on ensuring the wedding (OK, the first day) and the honeymoon (the first hundred days) are perfectly sunny. We send out a glowing announcement that this new person walks on water. We are all in and infatuated. They can do no wrong, and they have never done wrong. What a steal. We set up their new office to their personal style and liking. New carpet and stand-up desk. We carefully curate a first-day agenda and encourage the team to stop by their new office with best wishes or send a flowery welcome email. During the honeymoon, we are flexible and patient with them. We work hard to ensure they have all the support their heart desires to get those quick wins right out of the chute.

What do we do after the honeymoon? Year one? Year ten or year twenty? We moved our incoming junior in high school (yes, moving a kid in high school is never fun, and this is our second time), and he chose to interview at two potential preparatory schools (the expensive ones with boarding and day students; he is a day student). Talk about rolling out the carpet. Phone calls, videos, texts, swag, and gift sales from admissions, teachers, school leadership, and coaches. Talk about feeling wanted. We were so grateful for the attention because it made his transition much easier. Our son even commented that he never got the same attention from his old school and coaches after the first week of freshman year. They took him for granted after the honeymoon. We are all taken for granted, and we take others for granted at home and at work.

How do we re-recruit our team and show appreciation during the messy middle (i.e., everyday work life), whether after ninety days, a year, or decades? We should pay attention to those around us as we did when first recruiting them for the organization. Riding the rollercoaster of courting. This applies to marriages and kids as well, by the way. If you are a numbers person, research from Gallup has shown that replacing a solid employee costs up to two times the position's annual salary.[53] The Society for Human Resource Management says it takes an average of forty-two days to fill an open

---

53 Shane McFeely and Ben Wigert, "This Fixable Problem Costs U.S. Businesses $1 Trillion," Gallup, March 13, 2019, https://www.gallup.com/workplace/247391/fixable-problem-costs-businesses-trillion.aspx.

position and generally eight months for the replacement to become fully productive (talk about an extended honeymoon). Getting personal, divorcing individuals need more than a 30 percent increase in income to maintain the same standard of living[54] (not to mention having to manage the physical, emotional, and academic costs to them and their children).

Invest in the messy middle every day with your team. Pound the pavement to foster collaboration and teamwork. One last reminder that people leave bosses and teams. Get feedback on the work environment from formal surveys and check-ins with the team. Your monthly team meetings (or more frequent) are an opportunity to candidly talk about what needs work and what you (and the team) will do to fix it by the next meeting. Ensure they have the resources to do their job to their full potential. Remove barriers. Lend a helping hand where needed. Be flexible about how and where the work gets done (as long as it gets done). Provide opportunities for learning, growth, and development. This may be education at work, new projects, or furthering their formal education (certificates and advanced degrees). The diversity of the team matters. How you promote matters. Do internal candidates have a leg up over recruiting from the outside? There is a healthy tension here, but it is your responsibility as a leader to groom your team for growth. While money is not the top reason people become disengaged at work, we all have bills to pay. Stay attuned to compensation and benefits needs, wants, desires, and concerns directly with each team member. In summary, spend time with your team on all the little things. If you are effective with the little things, you have the foundation for success in all things.

---

54 Tamara Lytle, "When the Honeymoon's Over: Employee Engagement Tends to Wane over Time. You Can Intervene—and Keep the Spark Alive," *SHRM HR Quarterly*, August 1, 2012, https://www.shrm.org/topics-tools/news/hr-magazine/honeymoons.

After birth and everyday life, there is the end. Death. Facing our mortality. Fear of the unknown. When was the last time you attended a work funeral or work wake? After that big project failed miserably. We shut down that poorly performing business unit. Ending a product that was great until it wasn't. Transitioning a coworker, perhaps. Is there even such a thing?

Death—in life and in the office—is depressing and unsettling, filled with sadness and regrets. Death has connotations of loss, loss of control, nonexistence, and eternal punishment. Science has an authentic explanation for these feelings. "The brain does not accept that death is related to us," said Yair Dor-Ziderman at Bar-Ilan University in Israel. "We have this primal mechanism that means when the brain gets information that links self to death, something tells us it's not reliable, so we shouldn't believe it."[55] Our brains shield us from thinking about death. Death is something that happens to other people, not us. Thinking about death—let alone being OK with the dying process—goes against our core biology. We fight to stay alive, not die.

That is why most of us have an extraordinarily tough time ending things and getting rid of the places, people, and things that need to leave our lives. We should have let go of them long ago, but now they are stiff and smelling up the entire house. According to Dr. John Gottman, a professor emeritus at the University of Washington and expert on divorce prediction and marital stability, couples are unhappy for an average of six years before they are willing to get

55 Yair Dor-Ziderman et al., "Prediction-Based Neural Mechanisms for Shielding the Self from Existential Threat," *NeuroImage* 202 (2019): 116080, https://doi.org/10.1016/j.neuroimage.2019.116080.

help.[56] Think about that statistic for a moment. Letting go of our past. The things that don't matter anymore. Or never mattered in the first place. Accepting change and what is waiting anew out there.

The job that doesn't work. The boss and team members who don't work. Remember from that annual Gallup survey that 60 percent of the current workforce is disengaged. When we are disengaged, we "quiet quit." We come in later and leave earlier. We interact less with the team, relying on email, phone calls, and calendar requests. We would rather show our disenchantment with our workplace than quit to find greener pastures. There are no definitive statistics on how long it takes from an employee's initial disengagement to their eventual decision to quit a toxic work environment. The typical quit rate pre-pandemic was 1.6 percent. During the Great Resignation, it rose to 3 percent. Do the math for yourself—60 percent of the workplace is actively disengaged, while only 3 percent quit at the pinnacle of quitting.

How we end relationships is just as important as how we begin them. We let relationships decline, wilt, wither, deteriorate, and shrivel until they become noxious and malignant. We should get to these personal, team, and organizational cancers when they are in stage one (small and not spreading). Instead, we put off the crucial performance and behavior conversations until they reach stage four (where they have metastasized and spread to other relationships and team members, and this failed relationship affects all future relationships).

We should be far more intentional in ending things as gracefully as starting things. What we need are formal and fun organizational funerals and wakes. One last party to honor the death. Good endings

---

56 "The 6 Things That Predict Divorce: The First Step to Improving Your Marriage Is Understanding Why Relationships Fail," The Gottman Institute, accessed August 26, 2025, https://www.gottman.com/blog/the-6-things-that-predict-divorce/.

make for even better new beginnings. Ending things well affords us the luxury to pause and look back at what was. Uncover new things about ourselves, reflect on what we learned from experience, understand the "why" of what worked or didn't work, and assess (with deeper self-awareness) where we need to change existing and new relationships. An ending is not the end of it all. An ending is a beautiful chance to change and start something genuinely new.

Relationships are sacred. Well, at least at the beginning. "The Dash," a poignant poem written by Alton Maiden (a former Notre Dame scholar-athlete and now a teacher in his hometown of Dallas), was about what we get to do every day, not just what we have to do. In summary: "I've seen death staring me with my own eyes in a way many cannot know … After death has come and gone, a tombstone sits for many to see … Under the person's name, it reads the date of birth and the date the person passed … But thinking about the person, I can't help but remember the dash … Because people may forget your birth and death, but they will never forget your dash."[57]

We are all responsible for fully showing up from day one until the very last day. Fully accept others for what they are at their core. Appreciate them for who they are. Don't ever miss out on the parts that matter the most. Recognize when it is time for both of you to move on. And newly create with others in the next chapter. Be the "full hot orator" Brad Hamilton (Judge Reinhold) to Jeff Spicoli (Sean Penn) in *Fast Times at Ridgemont High* from 1982: "Right. Learn it. Know it. Live it." Think of it not as losing a job. But regaining a new life.

57 Lou Holtz, *Winning Every Day: The Game Plan for Success* (HarperCollins, 1999).

> *If you are the one who has to bid the necessary goodbye,* remember that your willingness to act with courage and compassion is what makes you distinct as a leader.
>
> *If you are the one who has been bid a necessary goodbye,* then remember that this decision is what you needed to find a place where you can put your unique skill set to better use. It might be a nudge to introspect and see whether there are things you could be doing differently.

No matter which camp you fall in, remember that you are at the threshold of transformation. Change has arrived at your doorstep. Will you step forward into this ending with the same intentionality you had at the beginning of this working relationship? Are you ready to choose courage over comfort? Are you ready to walk forward like the emu, like me? Are you ready to step into what's next with purpose?

ACKNOWLEDGMENTS

I would be remiss without starting by acknowledging my parents, Walter and Kathy. You were role models of faith, values, education, and service to others. To their mothers and my grandmothers, Alvira and Rose, I am eternally grateful for how you were my loudest cheerleaders while, at the same time, gracefully challenging me to reach my fullest potential. To my sisters and brothers in blood and marriage, I love you.

To my teachers at St. Frances Cabrini School (Piscataway, New Jersey), St. Joseph High School (Metuchen, New Jersey), the University of Notre Dame, and Cornell University, you fostered critical thinking, creativity, community engagement, and both the arts and the sciences. In that truly well-rounded education, you bestowed upon me and nurtured the gift of language and writing.

To my bosses, mentors, and colleagues in this true calling that we call healthcare leadership, you made me believe when I didn't believe. You never doubted when I doubted. You coached me in the basics while daring me to dream. Sister Marie de Pazzi. Gerry Tofani. Wayne Schiffner. Kevin Slavin. Chris Lutes. Beth O'Brien. Gus Blass. Rick Fleetwood. Jon Timmis. Brenda Simpson. Dean Sanpei.

Jennifer Wills. Seb "Eeyore" Girard. Dr. Scott Lichtenberger. Dr. Ozzie Grenardo. Leland Kaiser, Leanne Kaiser Carlson, Ryan Harris, and Kevin Kaiser. Last but not least … Eric Larsen.

To my executive coach, Don Hutton, you listened and guided me through my necessary goodbyes. More importantly, you encouraged me to put my thoughts and experiences on paper to be of service to the next generation of leaders.

To my professor in Composition and Literature from my freshman year, spring semester, who told me I was one of the worst writers they had ever seen and questioned how anyone could have let me into Notre Dame: I have a book.

ABOUT THE AUTHOR

Peter D. Banko is a transformational executive with nearly two decades of CEO-level experience leading complex, multifaceted health systems across the United States. He currently serves as president and CEO of Baystate Health, a not-for-profit integrated health system based in Western Massachusetts, and is known for leading organizations through exciting eras of healthy growth in business, community, and spirit.

Before joining Baystate Health in June 2024, Banko served as president and CEO of Centura Health, a joint operating agreement between national systems AdventHealth and CommonSpirit Health. During his tenure, he oversaw a $5.5 billion regional hospital and health services network that included over twenty-five owned and affiliated hospitals and a wide array of physician partnerships, clinics, and community-based services across Colorado, Kansas, and Utah.

A native of New Jersey, Banko found his calling in healthcare as a junior volunteer and rose through the ranks with a reputation for uprooting stagnant thinking and leading with passion and purpose. His teaching, supporting, and lifting those around him have influenced hospital operations, physician group alignment, and payer partnerships, making him a recognized leader in organizational transformation within the healthcare sector.

Banko earned his Bachelor of Business Administration from the University of Notre Dame and a Master of Health Administration from the prestigious Sloan Program in Health Services Administration at Cornell University. He continues to serve the industry as a thought leader and champion for purpose-driven leadership, human dignity, access, affordability, and the common good.

BIBLIOGRAPHY

1. Gallup, *State of the Global Workplace* (Gallup, 2022), https://www.gallup.com/workplace/349484/state-of-the-global-workplace-2022-report.aspx.

2. Jon Clifton, "Economic Growth Is Slowing: How Should Leaders Respond?" Gallup, June 12, 2023, https://www.gallup.com/workplace/506825/economic-growth-slowing-leaders-respond.aspx.

3. Ranjay Gulati and Eppa Rixey, "Nick Saban: Embracing 'The Process' of Sustaining Success," Harvard Business School Case 423-033, January 2023, revised August 2023, https://www.hbs.edu/faculty/Pages/item.aspx?num=63398.

4. The Week Staff, "George Steinbrenner, 1930–2010," *The Week*, January 9, 2015, https://theweek.com/articles/492741/george-steinbrenner-19302010.

5. Elena Lytkina Botelho et al., "What Sets Successful CEOs Apart," *Harvard Business Review*, May–June 2017, https://hbr.org/2017/05/what-sets-successful-ceos-apart.

6. QuotaPath, *2024 Sales Compensation Plan Report: Solving the Biggest Sales Compensation Challenges* (QuotaPath, 2024), https://www.quotapath.com/resource/report-solving-biggest-compensation-challenges/.

7. Mike Myatt, "10 Reasons Your Top Talent Will Leave You," *Forbes,* December 2012, https://www.forbes.com/sites/mikemyatt/2012/12/13/10-reasons-your-top-talent-will-leave-you/.

8. Jim Collins, *Good to Great: Why Some Companies Make the Leap … and Others Don't* (Harper Business, 2001).

9. Carl Gustav Jung, *The Archetypes and the Collective Unconscious* (Princeton University Press, 1980).

10. Substance Abuse and Mental Health Services Administration, *National Survey on Drug Use and Health (NSDUH)* (Substance Abuse and Mental Health Services Administration, 2022), https://www.samhsa.gov/data/data-we-collect/nsduh-national-survey-drug-use-and-health/national-releases/2022#annual-national-report.

11. Carol Dweck, *Mindset: The New Psychology of Success* (Ballantine Books, 2016).

12. Chloe Berger, "Satya Nadella Transformed Microsoft's Culture During His Decade as CEO by Transforming Everyone into 'Learn-It-Alls' Instead of 'Know-It-Alls'," *Fortune,* May 2024, https://fortune.com/2024/05/20/satya-nadella-microsoft-culture-growth-mindset-learn-it-alls-know-it-alls/.

13. "Ernesto 'Che' Guevara Quotes," QuotesData.com, accessed September 26, 2025, https://quotesdata.com/Ernesto_Guevara.html.

14. S&P Global Market Intelligence, *Global M&A by the Numbers: 2022 in Review* (S&P Global Market Intelligence, 2022), https://www.spglobal.com/market-intelligence/en/news-insights/research/global-ma-by-the-numbers-2022-in-review.

15. Christopher J. Goodman and Steven M. Mance, "Employment Loss and the 2007–09 Recession: An Overview," *Monthly Labor Review* 134, no. 4 (April 2011): 3-12, https://www.bls.gov/opub/mlr/2011/04/art1full.pdf.

16. Greg Iacurci, "2022 Was the 'Real Year of the Great Resignation,' Says Economist," CNBC, February 1, 2023, https://www.cnbc.com/2023/02/01/why-2022-was-the-real-year-of-the-great-resignation.html.

17. Douglas Adams, *The Hitchhiker's Guide to the Galaxy* (Harmony Books, 1980).

18. Sigmund Freud, *Civilization and Its Discontents* (W. W. Norton & Company, 2005).

19. "Sylvester Stallone Quotes," BrainyQuote, https://www.brainyquote.com/quotes/sylvester_stallone_584128.

20. Caroline Graham, "Hugh Grant Admits He's Nothing Like His Endearing On-Screen Roles," *Daily Mail*, August 27, 2016, https://www.dailymail.co.uk/news/article-3761656/I-annoyed-people-think-m-polite-Englishman-m-nasty-piece-work-freeze-hear-word-Action-Hugh-Grant-admits-s-like-endearing-screen-roles.html.

21. Mindy Weisberger, "'God Plays Dice with the Universe,' Einstein Writes in Letter About His Qualms with Quantum Theory," Live Science, June 12, 2019, https://www.livescience.com/65697-einstein-letters-quantum-physics.html.

22. Dante Alighieri, *The Divine Comedy: Inferno, Purgatory, and Paradise*, c. 1321.

23. Sharon Le Fort, "Stopping Self-Sabotage: How to Get Out of Your Own Way," *Sharon Le Fort*, April 9, 2023, https://sharonlefort.com.au/musings/f/stopping-self-sabotage.

24. National Center for Education Statistics, "Fast Facts: Home Schooling," accessed August 27, 2025, https://nces.ed.gov/fastfacts/display.asp?id=898.

25. National Institute of Mental Health, "Mental Illness," accessed August 27, 2025, https://www.nimh.nih.gov/health/statistics/mental-illness.

26. Scott Adams, *The Dilbert Principle: A Cubicle's-Eye View of Bosses, Meetings, Management Fads & Other Workplace Afflictions* (Harper Business, 1996).

27. Stephan Bisaha et al., "The Never-Ending Strike," NPR, January 5, 2023, https://www.npr.org/2023/01/05/1147120215/the-never-ending-strike.

28. Donald P. McNeill et al., *Compassion: A Reflection on the Christian Life* (Image Books, 1982).

29. D. Clark, "Average Company Lifespan of S&P 500 Companies 1965–2030," Statista, June 26, 2025, https://www.statista.com/statistics/1259275/average-company-lifespan/.

30. Mark Goodburn, "What Is the Life Expectancy of Your Company?" World Economic Forum, January 24, 2015, https://www.weforum.org/stories/2015/01/what-is-the-life-expectancy-of-your-company/.

31. Lila MacLellan, "It's Not Your Imagination. Women CEOs at Fortune 500 Companies Really Do Have Shorter Tenures Than Men," *Fortune*, February 20, 2024, https://fortune.com/2024/02/20/women-ceos-fortune-500-shorter-tenure-men/.

32. Robert K. Greenleaf, *Servant Leadership: A Journey into the Nature of Legitimate Power and Greatness* (Paulist Press, 1977).

33. "Uncontacted Tribes," Survival International, accessed August 26, 2025, https://www.survivalinternational.org/campaigns/uncontacted.

34. Colin R. M. Jackson et al., "Early Episodes of High-Pressure Core Formation Preserved in Plume Mantle," *Nature* 553, no. 7689 (2018): 491–495, https://doi.org/10.1038/nature25446.

35. Larry Bossidy, Ram Charan, and Charles Burck, *Execution: The Discipline of Getting Things Done* (Crown Business, 2002).

36. Robert Hogan and Joyce Hogan, "The Hogan Personality Inventory," in *Big Five Assessment*, ed. Boele de Raad and Marco Perugini (Hogrefe & Huber Publishers, 2002), 329–346.

37. Ron Carucci, "One More Time: Why Diversity Leads To Better Team Performance," *Forbes*, January 24, 2024, https://www.forbes.com/sites/roncarucci/2024/01/24/one-more-time-why-diversity-leads-to-better-team-performance/.

38. Doris Kearns Goodwin, *Team of Rivals: The Political Genius of Abraham Lincoln* (Simon & Schuster, 2005).

39. "Divorce Statistics: Over 115 Studies, Facts and Rates for 2024," Wilkinson & Finkbeiner Family Law Attorneys, accessed August 26, 2025, https://www.wf-lawyers.com/divorce-statistics-and-facts/.

40. "Teamwork Statistics 2024: Importance of Collaboration," TeamStage, accessed August 26, 2025, https://teamstage.io/teamwork-statistics/.

41. Gerald A. Michaelson and Steven W. Michaelson, *Sun Tzu—The Art of War for Managers: 50 Strategic Rules* (Adams Media, 2010).

42. Greenleaf, *Servant Leadership*.

43. "How Much Turnover Is Too Much?" Mercer, September 2025, https://www.imercer.com/articleinsights/workforce-turnover-trends.

44. Melanie Hughes, "How Executives Can Measure Success in the First Six Months," *Forbes*, January 2024, https://www.forbes.com/sites/melaniehughes/2024/01/18/how-executives-can-measure-success-in-the-first-6-months/.

45. "Leadership IQ Study: Why New Hires Fail," WorkComp Professionals, May 2010, https://www.workcompprofessionals.com/advisory/archive-0000/L5eBull2010/May/2010_05_a5.html.

46. Henry James, *The Portrait of a Lady* (Houghton, Mifflin and Company, 1881).

47. Brené Brown, *Dare to Lead* (Vermilion, 2018).

48. William Bridges, *Transitions: Making Sense of Life's Changes* (Hachette Books, 1980).

49. Christina Fang, Ji-Hyun (Jason) Kim, and Frances J. Milliken, "When Bad News Is Sugarcoated: Information Distortion, Organizational Search and the Behavioral Theory of the Firm," *Strategic Management Journal* 35, no. 8 (2014): 1186-1201, https://doi.org/10.1002/smj.2146.

50. Peter Senge, *The Fifth Discipline: The Art and Practice of the Learning Organization* (Doubleday/Currency, 1990).

51. Joseph Jaworski, *Synchronicity: The Inner Path of Leadership* (Berrett-Koehler Publishers, 2011).

52. Tom Morris, *If Aristotle Ran General Motors: The New Soul of Business* (Henry Holt and Company, 1997).

53. Shane McFeely and Ben Wigert, "This Fixable Problem Costs U.S. Businesses $1 Trillion," Gallup, March 13, 2019, https://www.gallup.com/workplace/247391/fixable-problem-costs-businesses-trillion.aspx.

54. Tamara Lytle, "When the Honeymoon's Over: Employee Engagement Tends to Wane over Time. You Can Intervene—and Keep the Spark Alive," *SHRM HR Quarterly*, August 1, 2012, https://www.shrm.org/topics-tools/news/hr-magazine/honeymoons.

55. Yair Dor-Ziderman et al., "Prediction-Based Neural Mechanisms for Shielding the Self from Existential Threat," *NeuroImage* 202 (2019): 116080, https://doi.org/10.1016/j.neuroimage.2019.116080.

56. "The 6 Things That Predict Divorce: The First Step to Improving Your Marriage Is Understanding Why Relationships Fail," The Gottman Institute, accessed August 26, 2025, https://www.gottman.com/blog/the-6-things-that-predict-divorce/.

57. Lou Holtz, *Winning Every Day: The Game Plan for Success* (HarperCollins, 1999).